DATE DUE

FEB 2 0 1996	
APR 1 9 1996	
APR 1 8 2001	

BRODART
Cat. No. 23-221

OUTPATIENT
TREATMENT
OF
SEX AND LOVE
ADDICTS

Outpatient Treatment of Sex and Love Addicts

Edited by
Eric Griffin-Shelley

Westport, Connecticut
London

Library of Congress Cataloging-in-Publication Data

Outpatient treatment of sex and love addicts / edited by
  Eric Griffin-Shelley.
      p.   cm.
    "Based on papers presented at the Annual Conference of the Eastern
  Psychological Association in New York in April 1991"—Introd.
    Includes bibliographical references (p.   ) and index.
    ISBN 0–275–94316–X (alk. paper)
    1. Sex addiction—Treatment—Congresses.   2. Relationship
  addiction—Treatment—Congresses.   I. Griffin-Shelley, Eric.
  RC560.S43I58   1993
  616.85'830651—dc20   92–18876

British Library Cataloguing in Publication Data is available.

Library of Congress Catalog Card Number: 92–18876
ISBN: 0–275–94316–X

First published in 1993

Praeger Publishers, 88 Post Road West, Westport, CT 06881
An imprint of Greenwood Publishing Group, Inc.

Printed in the United States of America

∞"

The paper used in this book complies with the Permanent
Paper Standard issued by the National Information Standards
Organization (Z39.48–1984).

10 9 8 7 6 5 4 3 2 1

Copyright Acknowledgment

The author and publisher are grateful to the following
for granting the use of material:

From *The Denial of Death* by Ernest Becker. Copyright ©
1973 by The Free Press, a Division of Macmillan, Inc.
Reprinted with the permission of the publisher.

Contents

Acknowledgments

I must begin by acknowledging my Higher Power, who daily graces me with understanding and inspiration in my work with sex and love addicts. Another source of daily strength and joy is my family—Helen and Griff—without whose love and support this project would not have been brought to completion.

My coworkers in the outpatient program deserve most of the credit for inspiring this volume. Their profound insights and dedicated work helped me to take the necessary steps to get their contributions to the point where they could be shared with the wider audience that they deserve.

Finally, I need to thank my clients, whose courage and commitment to recovery, despite the painful nature of the process, give me the strength, hope, and vision to carry on this important work.

OUTPATIENT
TREATMENT
OF
SEX AND LOVE
ADDICTS

CHAPTER 1

Introduction

Eric Griffin-Shelley

Sex and love addiction is a relatively new conception for understanding and treating compulsive sexual behavior and relationship dependency. This approach to obsessive, driven sexual acting out and intensive, unending, and unhealthy romantic attachments has grown out of addiction recovery and treatment. The founder of the Augustine Fellowship of Sex and Love Addicts Anonymous (SLAA) discovered that his sexual compulsivity did not settle down (as he anticipated it would) when he established sobriety from alcohol with the help of Alcoholics Anonymous (AA). Consequently, in 1976 he began meetings for people with obsessive relationship and sexual acting-out problems based on the Twelve Steps of AA. His ability to deal with one compulsion through the support and direction of a Twelve Step program led him to believe that the same principles and practices might work for difficulties with sexual activities that were out of control and relationships that were unmanageable.

Other recovering people had the same idea, and other Twelve Step programs grew up in different sections of the United States. The Midwest saw the development of Sex Addicts Anonymous (SAA). On the West Coast, Sexaholics Anonymous (SA) was founded. Sexual Compulsives Anonymous (SCA) was started in New York City. Each of these separate fellowships applied the Twelve Steps of AA to problems with compulsive sexuality.

At the same time that recovering people were applying the lessons of Twelve Step recovery to sex and love, professionals who work with addicted clients began to think and write about sex and love as addictions.

In 1975, Stanton Peele and Archie Brodsky published *Love and Addiction*. In the 1980s, a number of books appeared, including the landmark work of Patrick Carnes, *Out of the Shadows: Understanding Sexual Addiction* (1983), and Robin Norwood's best selling *Women Who Love Too Much: When You Keep Wishing and Hoping He'll Change* (1985). Since the ground-breaking work presented in these volumes, there have been a half a dozen other efforts to examine either love dependencies or sexual compulsivity. In 1991, the editor of this book published *Sex and Love: Addiction Treatment and Recovery*, which integrated both sexual acting out and romantic obsessions in one theoretical framework similar to that of SLAA.

Treatment programs and professional training efforts have been developed since 1985. The first inpatient treatment program for sex addiction was at the Golden Valley Health Center in Golden Valley, Minnesota. That state is responsible for the "Minnesota model" of chemical dependency treatment, which includes such elements as the 28-day residential treatment program, so it is not surprising that it had the first residential treatment facility for sex addicts.

The University of Minnesota's Continuing Medical Education program started the National Conference on Sexual Compulsivity/Addiction, and in 1991 the fourth national meeting of this conference focused on all aspects of sexual compulsivity/addiction. The name of the conference suggests the split in the professional community regarding the proper approach to treatment of out-of-control sexual behaviors. Some professionals, usually those with sex therapy backgrounds, advocate a cognitive/behavioral approach to treatment and disagree with the conceptualization of sexual behaviors as addictions. Other professionals, often those with chemical dependency treatment backgrounds, prefer to use the Twelve Step approach to recovery and frequently advocate the "disease model" approach seen in most chemical dependency programs. Nonetheless, efforts to educate and to expand treatment availability are being seen in local and regional conferences and in the development of programs such as the outpatient program presented in this book.

This book is based on papers presented at the annual conference of the Eastern Psychological Association held in New York in April 1991. At this panel presentation, the authors presented many aspects of our outpatient program for sex and love addicts. In Chapter 2, Griffin-Shelley gives a definition of sex and love addiction that includes important diagnostic criteria such as the "high," tolerance, dependence, withdrawal, cravings, obsession, compulsion, secrecy, and personality change/dissociation. He indicates how these aspects of sex and love addiction interrelate and create a pattern that can be labeled an addiction. He then describes the therapeutic program that he developed to work with people who suffer from this disease.

William Lord expands Griffin-Shelley's diagnostic considerations in Chapter 3, "A Diagnostic Proposal with Neurochemical Underpinnings." He makes an informed and articulate plea for the development of diagnostic classifications for "behavioral disorders" that include addictions to activities such as sex or exercise as well as the traditional addictions to chemicals. He explains the neurochemical link between all of these addictions in a way that is readily understandable and convincing.

Chapter 4, "Using Individual and Group Therapy in Recovery," was prepared by Griffin-Shelley in conjunction with Helen Griffin-Shelley, a social worker in private practice. It looks at the different therapeutic approaches that can be used to promote recovery from sex and love addiction, especially individual and group therapy. The strengths and weaknesses of each are presented with case examples to illustrate the positive and negative values of each.

Jeffrey Kaufman, the outpatient program coordinator and a group leader, reviews "Group Process Issues in Men's Groups" in Chapter 5. In it, he reviews group membership and identity, group rituals, the issue of outside contact, and sexual abstinence. In addition, he comments on father issues, shame and narcissistic vulnerability, shame and the group therapist, and closeness and distance among group members. He closes with a review of dissociative trends and mirroring.

Chapter 6 was prepared by Linda Dubrow, who led an ongoing group for women sex and love addicts and also did some work with codependents. In "Women's Issues in Recovery," she considers special diagnostic concerns for women that center on love dependency and sexual acting out. She elaborates by defining the population more clearly and discussing the benefits of same-sex group therapy. She also looks at resistance to treatment for women and their families and at multiple addictions, especially sex and love together with food and spending, as they relate to the recovery of women sex and love addicts. With these clients the issue of pregnancy risk is of special note, as are the histories of childhood trauma and incest. Dubrow concludes with some comments on separation/individuation and using relationship-based therapy to treat people with relationship problems.

Another of our group therapists, Steve Heilakka, who also has his own therapy practice, has developed some ideas about "Integrating Sex Therapy and Addiction Recovery" in Chapter 7. He begins with the idea that sexuality can meet a variety of needs, including inner child needs from our past, adult needs in our present, and spiritual needs for our future. The intense power of our sexuality can also lead to feelings of terror and awe. Heilakka reflects on the impact of Victorian and Puritanical heritages on our views of sexuality and the emphasis on the act of sex rather than on sexuality. Such a sex-negative approach leads to objectification, dependency, and shame. Healthy sexuality has a sex-positive view that emphasizes the process and developmental issues. Similarly, Twelve Step fellowships for sexual compulsives advocate a sex-positive view that focuses on relationships and spirituality, and downplays the importance of the act of sex. He then takes sexual addiction a bit further and looks at it as a symptom of childhood sexual trauma. He explains how a Twelve Step approach allows for the necessary safety, boundaries, corrective emotional experiences, learning about intimacy and relationships, and attention to the inner child that will produce recovery and healing.

Finally, Steve Dubrow-Eichel rounds out the material in Chapter 8, discussing "The Cultural Context of Sex and Love Addiction Recovery" from his vantage point as a quasi-neutral observer of our program. He offers some personal and insightful examples of love obsessions and compulsive sexuality that reveal problems with impulse control, dissociative states, and compulsive behaviors with chemicals as well as sex and love. He then looks at four different antecedents to sex and love addictions: psychobiological, cultural, existential, and psychological. He points out our inherent need for transcendent or "peak" experiences. He examines the "Me Decade" and its paradoxical lack of control and efforts to take control. Addictions promise to relieve our numbness, detachment, and fragmentation. Our grandiosity and cultural narcissism also point to an escape or temporary transcendence. In individuals, the psychological problems of shame and dissociation can be predisposing factors in the development of an addiction. He compellingly pulls all of this together in the final concept of our modern day hero as a "spiritual warrior."

The book ends with comments by Griffin-Shelley that attempt to summarize the contributions of the authors and to point toward the future of sex and love addiction treatment and recovery. He looks at some trends that indicate the convergence of various specialty areas in psychology. Work in the area of posttraumatic stress disorders, developments with obsessive/compulsive disorders, progress in chemical dependency, and therapy for sexual trauma and multiple personality disorders all seem to be coming together and to be necessary for work with clients who have sex and love addictions. He illustrates this with a case example and encourages clinicians to have hope, determination, and understanding in dealing with this sometimes baffling and always challenging disorder.

CHAPTER 2

Sex and Love Addiction: Definition and Overview

Eric Griffin-Shelley

Professionals and recovering people have struggled with definitions of addictions for years. The root of the word "addiction" is *ad dictum* ("to the dictator"). When people were conquered long ago, they were sent *ad dictum* (to the dictator), where they were slaves without freedom or any control over their lives. Addiction, then, means slavery. Addicts themselves identify with this loss of choice or freedom. When they are "hooked," they are not free to choose to stop whatever addictive behavior they have. Alcoholics are not free to stop drinking. Gamblers feel they have no choice but to gamble. Sex and love addicts feel compelled to act out in sexual or romantic ways as if they had lost their freedom of choice.

This question of whether an addict really has a choice, is really free, is the crux of much of the debate about how the addict can change. In Twelve Step recovery programs, the First Step is to "admit powerlessness" over the drug or activity to which one is addicted. Many people find this troubling because there appears to be a clear choice by the addict to engage in the addicting activity. No one can force someone to drink, eat, spend, exercise, or make love to excess unless there is some willingness on the part of the individual. The subjective experience of most addicts, however, is quite the opposite. They may have had a choice early in their abuse of the chemical or the activity, but as their addiction has progressed, they feel less and less in control and able to say "no" to the urge to participate in the activity. Addicts feel like slaves to drink, drugs, food, sex, money, or whatever their individual demon is.

Thus, a simple definition of addiction might be enslavement to a chemical or an activity. Another, more clinical way of saying this would be that an addiction is a *pathological relationship with an experience that causes damage to the person.* By "pathological" I mean unhealthy and out of balance. Addicts are people of extremes, and addictions are characterized by extreme behaviors. Our bodies seek homeostasis or balance. When something goes out of balance, our bodies automatically seek to regain their equilibrium. Pathology, then, is being sick and out of balance. A pathological relationship is an unhealthy and out-of-balance involvement or connection.

This unbalanced contact is with some type of experience. The experience may be taking drugs or drinking alcohol, but it could just as easily be running, working out, eating, working, spending, praying, confessing, cleaning, trying to be perfect, or even doing the crossword puzzle. In other words, we have come to realize that it is not necessary to ingest a chemical to have an addiction. In fact, many activities create "good feeling" chemicals in our brains such as endorphins and it may be these we get hooked on when we don't take drugs or drink. Thus, all types of experience may have the potential to create a good feeling (based on a chemical change in the brain) and therefore be potentially addicting.

Addictions do not involve positive, creative interactions with experiences. Instead, an addiction causes damage to the person who is hooked. So, in addition to being pathological relationships to experiences, addictions are destructive and not life enhancing. For most addicts, the initial involvement is not damaging. A person can smoke marijuana, overeat, gamble, make love, or pray without getting addicted. In fact, most people who have the experience will not become addicted to it. Usually only 5–15 percent of those who have an experience become obsessed with it and engage in compulsive rituals of use and abuse. For an addict, however, there is a point at which the experience begins to cause damage and the addict continues to engage in the behavior. This seems to be where rationality leaves off and addiction begins. This is the line that is crossed which makes an alcoholic "powerless" or unable to choose while a "social drinker" can stop and not continue to be hurt by the experience.

One way to define addictions and put them in a context that will make clear the differences between avoidance, use, abuse, and addiction is to think of the bell curve in mathematics. The bell curve represents the normal distribution of any event, activity, habit, or experience. An example follows (see Figure 2.1). Using this schema, a person's relationship to any experience can be placed somewhere under the curve from the extreme left—a complete abhorrence or avoidance of the experience (e.g., the

Figure 2.1
Example of a Bell Curve

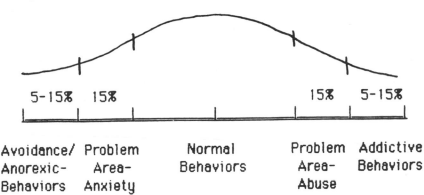

| 5-15% | 15% | | | 15% | 5-15% |

Avoidance/	Problem	Normal	Problem	Addictive
Anorexic-	Area-	Behaviors	Area-	Behaviors
Behaviors	Anxiety		Abuse	

anorexic's horror of eating)—to the extreme right—an intense, obsessive, compulsive involvement with the experience (e.g., the overeater's love affair with food). In terms of sex and love, some people are extremely fearful and avoidant of romantic and/or sexual encounters; on the other hand, others are totally preoccupied with sexuality and/or love to the point where nothing else seems to matter.

In addition to these two extremes, there are people who have problems with sex and love but are not anorexic or addicted. Some people are afraid of sex and love but have some tenuous contact with these experiences; others are infatuated with romance and sexuality but are able to stop short of addiction. At either end, roughly 20–30 percent of the population fall into the anorexic/avoidant or problematic group or the addicted or almost out-of-control group. This means that the middle group under the curve— the sexually and romantically balanced people—account for anywhere from 40 to 60 percent. In simple terms, as many as one person in three is on one end of the continuum, one in three is at the other end, and one falls in the middle.

Defining addictions and addictive behaviors can be a complex and difficult task, especially when seeking to do clinical research or to establish consistency in the application of a definition. So far, we have taken a rather broad and all-encompassing view. A more specific definition calls for a more focused and detailed examination of the phenomena. Although great specificity is not possible in this discussion, I will review the definition of sex and love addiction presented in my book *Sex and Love: Addiction Treatment and Recovery* (1991). Sex and love addiction includes nine elements: the "high," tolerance, dependence, cravings, withdrawal, obsession, compulsive behaviors, secrecy, and personality change. A sex and love addict need not have all of the elements in order to qualify as an addict but anyone who has more than three of the elements should consider himself or herself, or be considered by others, a possible sex and love addict. The more elements are present and the more intense each element is, the more likely the person is a sex and love addict. In the next few pages, I will outline these elements in greater detail.

THE HIGH

In order to get hooked on something, there needs to be a good feeling—a "fix" or a high. Most of us are familiar with the excitement of sexuality or the glow of love. Most of us look at these experiences with fondness and desire to recapture or re-create these feelings as often as we can. However, most people do not become slaves to this high and feel that life is not worth living if we do not have a certain sexual conquest, romantic liaison, or passionate outlet. The sex and love addict is constantly searching for that one person, that one experience which will allow him or her to transcend pain and find peace and fulfillment. They have many such encounters, and each contact in some way reinforces the continuation of their efforts to find more, better, longer-lasting grasps of heaven, of that good-feeling fix, of that natural high.

Some people see the good feeling as necessarily orgasmic. In fact, sexual activity itself may be only a small part of the high that the sex and love addict pursues. Most sex and love addicts spend a great deal of time in preoccupation and fantasy before they act out. A love-addicted woman would spend hours each week planning her outfit, her conversation, her hair, and her perfume for an affair that occupied perhaps an hour on Friday afternoons. A lawyer sex addict spent so many hours each day in fantasy that he eventually lost his job through lack of productivity. Sex and love addicts love to spend hours cruising, intriguing, and trying to "score." The chase may be much more exciting and challenging than the sexual act itself, which often leads to despair and self-hatred after it is over and the reality of acting out crashes in, to the horror of the sex and love addict.

TOLERANCE

Tolerance is commonly associated with alcohol and drug use. The idea is that our bodies accommodate to ingested chemicals and, as a result of this adaptation by our physiology, we need more of the chemical to produce the desired effect. I might get drunk on one beer if I never drank before, but after I have "learned to drink" and can "hold my liquor," I can have two or three beers and not feel the effect. This is tolerance.

Sex and love addicts develop similar patterns of tolerance to their own levels of excitement or arousal and to the stimuli that "turn them on." Over time, they need more and more, or more exotic or erotic, forms of activity or stimulation, in order to produce the same fix or high. An example would be persons who masturbate compulsively. They might not need much to get aroused initially and might be satisfied after masturbating once. After a while, though, they tend to need more graphic forms of written or visual stimuli, and can need to masturbate 10 or 15 times a day. In other words, their tolerance has grown so high that they will not be satisfied with masturbating once or twice a day. Similarly, love addicts may find that they need more and more attention, devotion, gifts, or signs of loyalty from their partner. They may not be satisfied with their lover's statements of faithfulness and commitment, and may feel drawn to follow the person, to check on his or her whereabouts and company, to threaten suicide or physical harm in order to get the level of intensity in the relationship that they need in order to feel fulfilled.

DEPENDENCE

Again, the field of chemical dependency is the model for the concept of dependence. Drugs such as heroin, alcohol, and nicotine produce a physiological dependence. That is, the body builds up a tolerance to these drugs and begins to expect a daily supply. When the daily dose of the chemical is not present, the body starts to get sick and to go into a withdrawal syndrome. Other drugs, like marijuana, cocaine, and amphetamines, produce a serious psychological dependence, but they do not have the same physiological dependency syndrome.

Sex and love addictions are more similar to the stimulant-type drugs in their production of a dependency syndrome, that is, the dependence tends to be primarily a psychological one rather than a physiological one. There may be a neurochemical basis for the psychological dependency, but the exact nature of this underlying chemical action is not yet known. The psychological dependency is the most troubling aspect of chemical dependency in any case, so the presence or absence of a "true" physiological dependency may be of little value at this point in our understanding of addictions. Those of us who work in the field of chemical dependency know that we can get someone physically clean—no longer physiologically dependent—in three to five days. Staying away from a life-style that includes a dependency on drugs and/or alcohol takes much longer. The same is true for sex and love addicts. Learning alternative ways of meeting their psychological dependency needs instead of using sex or romance for a quick fix is a long and difficult task.

CRAVINGS

Addicts of all types experience cravings—sudden, intense urges to have a particular type of experience. These cravings are often the cause of "slips, trips, and falls" along the road to recovery and may lead to relapse if not attended to. Cravings are particularly troublesome because they seem to come without warning. However, with some proper education and training about triggers and how cravings are "set up" by the addict, most addicts can prevent a craving from becoming an opportunity to act out. Cravings will continue long after addicts' recovery programs are under way—although the intensity of the desire will lessen over time. These sudden impulses to indulge in the "forbidden fruit" may be with the addict for the rest of his or her life, especially if the addiction has worn a deep groove or habit pattern in the addict's personality.

Many sex and love addicts compare their cravings to the intense urges that cocaine addicts report—even after relatively long periods of sobriety. Usually sex and love addicts experience a feeling that may seem to overwhelm them at least momentarily, and at this point they need to act quickly to ensure their abstinence. A craving that is entertained for long in the body or mind usually becomes a reality in terms of being acted out.

WITHDRAWAL

Like other addicts, sex and love addicts, when they cease indulging their cravings and no longer give in to their impulses, experience a period of withdrawal. There appears to be a physiological adjustment that needs to be gone through which may include disturbed sleep and appetite, difficulty concentrating, agitation or low energy level, and anhedonia or lack of pleasure in the normal aspects of life. Their physical complaints or other somatic difficulties may last two to six weeks.

The more difficult aspect of the withdrawal is the psychological part. Most addicts experience intense feelings of tension, anxiety, anger, irritability, sadness, emptiness, boredom, hopelessness, helplessness, and depression. These feelings may be very frightening and unnerving, especially if they are unexpected and overwhelming. Some sex and love addicts benefit from an antidepressant medication during this period. The withdrawal tends to last between one and three months but can be longer, depending on a number of variables: slips, the amount of support available, and the commitment of the addict.

OBSESSION

Addictions seem to create people with obsessions and compulsions. In fact, there may be neurochemical similarities between addicts and people who suffer from obsessive/compulsive disorder. An obsession is a persistent, intrusive thought that persons cannot seem to get out of their minds even when they want to eliminate it. Sex and love addicts tend to get stuck thinking about sex and/or romance for long periods of time. Even when they have decided to put an end to endless fantasies and preoccupations, they often find that they cannot turn off their minds. The more they struggle not to think sexual and/or romantic thoughts, the more these thoughts push themselves to the forefront of their minds. Sex and love addicts have used their obsessions as ways to nurture themselves and to numb the pain in their lives, so when it comes time to give up their obsessive thoughts, they feel like they are losing an important and valuable part of themselves.

Obsessions are important aspects of the addictive process, and most addicts spend much more time thinking about sex and love than they actually spend being sexual or loving. Obsessive thought patterns create strong and deep habit patterns within the cognitive and coping structures of the person, and tend to remain ruts that are easy to fall back into, especially in the early stages of the recovery process.

COMPULSION

Compulsions are the expression in action of obsessions. After a period of thinking about being sexual or romantic, sex and love addicts often feel overwhelmed and compelled to act out their fantasies. Compulsive behaviors have an impulsive and out-of-control quality although they may appear to be calculated and thought out. What usually happens is that sex and love addicts will begin a ritual after an obsession, and during this ritualized behavior they will enter an almost trancelike state. In this depersonalized and detached ego state, they are able to do things that they would not do in a more normal state of consciousness. Addicts themselves refer to this trancelike state as "being in my addict," almost as if the addict part of them had taken over and there were not other parts capable of intervening with the compulsion to be sexual or relational.

A great many sex and love addicts have experienced severe trauma in their childhoods and consequently have developed the capacity to detach, depersonalize, and take on different ego states even though they may not actually have multiple personalities. These people are, then, often quite able to experience trancelike ego states after performing certain rituals. For example, an exhibitionist who knows that his behavior is hurtful to others will start "cruising" after a period of fantasy and preoccupation, and as a result will "get into my addict," act out, and then feel terrible when he returns to a more normal ego state. Love addicts may listen to music, dress up, and have fantasy conversations as a prelude to acting out in terms of romantic yet destructive relationships.

SECRECY

Most addicts try to hide their obsessions and compulsions. For instance, an alcoholic may have a few drinks before going to a party so as not to appear to be drinking too much. Sex and love addicts are the most secretive of addicts. Our culture seems to teach us that we should not be open about our sexuality, and most of us are quite hesitant to talk about what our sex lives are really like. Thus, sex is a secret in our society and, consequently, those who are experiencing difficulty being in control of their sexual and romantic thoughts and behaviors feel terribly ashamed and embarrassed at having such a problem. There is a great stigma to having a sexual problem of some sort, and people frequently joke that they would like to "catch" some sexual addiction. This deep sense of shame leads sex and love addicts to lead secret lives.

I have frequently had clients come to me and tell me that their spouse or family has no idea that they have a sex and love addiction problem. Most of my clients have had great success keeping this secret for years. In fact, the issue of involving family or spouse in the treatment process is often a very difficult one because the sex and love addict has been so successful at keeping the other life a secret for so long. Professionals have come to me with long histories of involvement in pornography, masturbation, adult bookstores, and prostitutes that have never come to light. Love addicts have managed to have multiple affairs and sometimes even multiple marriages and families without their partners knowing what they have been up to.

PERSONALITY CHANGE

Addicts often seem to transform into other personalities under the influence of their addictive experience. It is quite common for families of alcoholics to say, "He's so sweet and kind when he's sober, and when he's drinking, he's the meanest, rottenest man you could ever meet." Sex and love addicts show the same patterns of personality changes, but the influence of their "drug" is not as obvious. They are warm, loving, kind, and exciting at one time and cold, manipulative, detached, and harsh at another time without any apparent reason for their differing moods. Often, during the good periods, they are filled with guilt and shame over their acting out and tend to overcompensate, trying to make up for not being available or caring while they were acting out. In their bad moods, they are "in their addict" and seem only to care about themselves and their own satisfaction.

Addictions also tend to reinforce certain personality characteristics like impulsivity, narcissism, instant gratification, infantile demands, avoidance of pain, and a "quick fix" mentality. The addict's personality may be transformed over time into more and more of what those in Twelve Step programs call "His Majesty the Baby," a person who wants what he wants when he wants it. This change in personality may be quite subtle and gradual, but over time, those who know the person will begin to see him or her as "no longer himself/herself," or, at least some of the time, as apparently someone other than the person they know and care about.

A complex definition of sex and love addiction, then, would include all of the elements outlined above: the high, tolerance, dependence, craving, withdrawal, obsession, compulsion, secrecy, and personality change. In order to qualify as a sex and love addict, a person probably needs to have symptoms in at least three of these areas. The more symptoms the person has and the more severe the symptoms are, the more serious and potentially lethal the disease.

Sex and love addicts can be of any age, either sex, and from any economic group. As with other addictions, sex and love addiction knows no limits nor boundaries as far as these demographic variables go. There appear to be no limits of race, ethnic group, or social class. In other words, sex and love addicts are both rich and poor, intelligent and not so smart, black and white, teenagers and elderly, professionals and working class, and heterosexual and homosexual. All of the in-between groups also have sex and love addicts: the middle class, the average intelligence, other racial groups, the middle-aged, the average worker, and the bisexual. Since sexuality and relationships are issues for all human beings, all of us are vulnerable to developing this illness.

─────────── **AN OUTPATIENT THERAPY PROGRAM** ───────────

The final segment of Chapter 2 is a description of an intensive outpatient therapy program designed to treat patients who qualify for diagnosis as sex and love addicts. This program was developed in the fall of 1988 to meet the needs of a growing number of clients who were coming forward and identifying themselves as sex and love addicts. Initially, these patients had been treated with individual psychotherapy and attendance at Sex and Love Addicts Anonymous (SLAA) meetings. While this approach seemed to work for some, many needed a more intensive therapeutic intervention to help them identify and maintain "bottom line" behaviors and to begin recovering from this difficult and embarrassing addiction.

A three-and-a-half hour evening program was designed with three basic elements: psychoeducational groups, same-sex group psychotherapy, and Twelve Step meetings. Alcoholics and other addicts have learned over the years that bibliotherapy (Griffin-Shelley, 1990) can help to initiate, develop, and sustain a recovery process from an addictive disorder. Reading is educating oneself about the nature of the disorder and ways of coping with it. Our premise is that recovery begins with education. Most self-help and rehabilitation programs likewise emphasize the importance of the recovering person's learning about the disease. In addition to educating the consumer, the placement of the psychoeducational group first proved to be a good stimulus to the group therapy sessions that followed. The lectures often worked like a "warm-up" exercise for psychodrama or a daily orientation program to what the goals were for the therapy and recovery process that the evening was designed to support.

PSYCHOEDUCATIONAL GROUPS

The formats of the psychoeducational groups vary a great deal, depending on the presenter and the topic. The program supervisor and all of the group therapists take turns leading the psychoeducational groups. Sometimes the session is a regular lecture with a written handout and use of a blackboard. Other times, the group meets in a circle and holds a discussion. Other variations include use of dyads and triads, breaking into small groups, role-playing, and psychodrama. We incorporate brainstorming and evaluation techniques as well as other types of structured activities for small groups.

The topics of the sessions cover a broad range, but they all relate to the overall goal: recovery from sex and love addictions. Some psycho-educational sessions have covered adult sexuality, tools of recovery, grieving and forgiving, self-esteem, and communication skills. Others focused on shame, meditation, equal relations, getting in touch with the inner child, bottom-line behaviors, triggers, and boundaries. Sessions were given on depression, cross addictions, relationships in the SLAA program, male and female roles, types of therapy, overeating, and spirituality. Codependency, healthy relationships, nurturing, the addiction cycle, the disease concept, and core beliefs were addressed. We also looked at giving feedback, powerlessness, stress, separating from your family of origin, and incest (covert and overt). Other topics were "came to believe . . . ," stages of normal development, ego defenses and roles we play, love dependency and healthy love. Finally, secrecy, affirmations, illusions and fantasies, and replacing old habits with new ones were discussed. In addition to these many and varied topics, each of the Twelve Steps is reviewed in detail. Opportunities are given for clients to share their own experiences, to ask questions in a safe environment, and to get feedback in most of these sessions, since their participation in such activities will enhance the likelihood of learning.

The psychoeducational sessions are of value in many ways. The session is generally less threatening than group therapy because the focus does not have to be on the individual unless he or she chooses to be the person who is sharing. The group is larger than the therapy groups, so that there is safety in numbers and it is easier to be an active listener without feeling pressured to participate. Psychoeducational groups also help to develop positive coping skills such as listening and thinking. Sex and love addicts are accustomed to ignoring others and responding to impulses, so the structure and format encourage the engagement of their intellectual and rational abilities. In short, psychoeducation reinforces the recovery message: think before you act. In the obsessive/compulsive cycle of the sex and love addict, thinking has been replaced by fantasizing about sexual and romantic encounters. In recovery, this process needs to be reversed; addicts need to retrain their minds to think realistically, rationally, and reasonably about their feelings and impulses.

Sometimes there is resistance to this approach because it has echoes of earlier school environments that may have lowered the sex and love addicts' sense of self-worth. Some clients have learning disabilities or a history of school failure that can be triggered simply by the arrangement of the chairs in a lecture format. Efforts are made to address these inhibitions and to create a supportive, engaging educational experience that can counterbalance any fears or resistances to learning by varying the structure of the sessions as well as the arrangement of the room.

GROUP PSYCHOTHERAPY

After a ten-minute break, the participants divide into smaller group psychotherapy sessions that last for an hour and a half. The groups are separated by sex, and the leader is of the same sex as the group members. Opening up about a sex and love addiction can surface a great deal of shame, embarrassment, anxiety, and self-hatred. The group needs to be a safe place. The small numbers (maximum of seven members, usually six) and same-sex composition seem to facilitate this objective. Most of the group members are relieved to know that they will be in a same-sex group, especially in the early stages of recovery. Part of the rationale for same-sex therapy groups is to reduce the likelihood of triggering sex and love addictive fantasies and desires among the group members. This, of course, does not account for homosexual orientations, but since the group has both heterosexual and homosexual members, this seems to be a manageable problem. Most SLAA meetings are open to both sexes, so the group setting may be the safest place for someone to learn how to be open and honest.

The style or therapeutic orientation of the groups is basically traditional group psychotherapy. While the group leaders have had varying professional training, the goals of the groups are the same: to facilitate learning to open up, to develop new coping skills like honesty, to get feedback (or "cross talk," which is banned from SLAA meetings) from peers, to receive affirmation of the person's value and worth, to learn to have healthy peer relationships, and to allow others to offer support and caring. The groups are also designed to offer the chance for cathartic emotional experiences, for reparenting and contacting the "inner child," and for improving the ability to experience and understand nonsexual intimacy.

Sex and love addicts are actually very lonely people. Earle, Crow, and Osborn entitled their book on sex addiction *Lonely All the Time* (1989). While most are quite frightened of group psychotherapy, they also know that their interpersonal relationships need improvement. Usually, after initial avoidance or anxiety, they become quite attached; our groups have enjoyed a stability of membership and loyalty unlike what we have seen with other addicts, especially chemically dependent clients. Most sex and love addicts have had abusive, neglectful, or damaging relationships with their families that need to be worked on in a group setting in order to experience healthier contacts with people that are nurturing but respectful, affirming but challenging, caring but confrontational. They may need to share with others—perhaps for the first time—the real nature of their early life experiences and to work through some of the trauma in order to be able to trust others and to allow themselves to have contact and intimacy. Individual therapy may be too threatening for some clients due to incestuous relationships or enmeshment, so the group therapy situation can be a place for initial healing before this can be done in a one-to-one relationship.

The groups all begin with the same format. The members and the therapist say, "We come together in this group to get honest with ourselves and each other; what is said in the group stays in the group; honesty is the key to sobriety." These are the basic ground rules for the group: honesty and confidentiality. Addicts live lives of secrecy and shame. If this is to be changed, they need to learn to be honest. The group also has to be a safe place. Most addicts have not had a safe place. They may have searched frantically for safe, loving partners, or they may have seen their safety in acting out, but in the long run, neither of these worked and they ended up alone and scared. Coming together on a weekly basis with commitment and consistency can start to build the healthy bonds that are the basis for the trust and intimacy that they so desperately desire. We do not have a lot of other rules, like no socializing outside the group. In fact, we look at contacts between group meetings as supportive and helpful to individual recovery and indicative of group development.

The formats of the groups vary somewhat, with the biggest difference being the ways they structure their time. Usually they start with a brief (two–three minutes) opening statement from each member that is frequently a comment about how the week went or how recovery is going. One group carefully limits the time, with each person being allotted about 10 minutes to speak and a few minutes for group members to give feedback; another group lets members talk as long as they need. This means that in some groups, each person gets to talk each week, while in other groups only three or four people may have the time to talk each time. The decision about the way that time is used is up to each group, and they have developed their own styles in this area.

The groups end with a closing statement from each person and the therapist that usually summarizes the person's experience in the group that evening or the current state of resolution of the problem he or she discussed that evening. One of the groups closes by standing, holding hands, and saying, "We raise our eyes from shame to grace (meanwhile looking up to each other from an initial downward gaze)," followed by the Serenity Prayer: "God, grant me the serenity to accept the things I cannot change, the courage to change the things I can, and the wisdom to know the difference." Other groups simply end after the closing statements. For the group that holds hands, the decision to make physical contact with one another was not a simple or easy one. In SLAA there is a "no physical contact" rule because of the possibility that sexual intrigue, games, seduction, and acting out may be triggered by touching. In addition to this danger, many sex and love addicts have been sexually abused or have had abusive relationships that involved violations of personal boundaries such as physical space.

The group psychotherapy is seen by the patients as the most important aspect of the evening program. Many can find other ways to learn what we review in the psychoeducational sessions, but they cannot find the safety, consistency, openness, and support for healing and building relational skills anywhere else. Their group is very important to them because it provides a place to check themselves out in terms of their own honesty and recovery process. The weekly sessions provide a certain accountability, something usually quite lacking in an active sex and love addict's life. Their group also functions as a nurturing environment that can help them work through some of the hurt and damage of their past. Group is a place where they can test new ideas, behaviors, coping skills, and ways of thinking without having to take the risks that would be involved with other people in their daily lives. Their group will also tell them when they are off track or in dangerous territory, which many of them never hear from others or hear only when it is self-serving or codependent. Group therapy provides a reality check, a source for affirmations of progress, and a place to take their troubles and heartaches. In short, the group psychotherapy has many goals and serves many functions in the recovery process.

TWELVE STEP MEETING

At the end of our intensive evening program, there is a meeting of SLAA that is open to the public. We originally had some difficulty in establishing this meeting because of the issue of independence. SLAA, as a Twelve Step program, has traditions that state "A S.L.A.A. group ought never endorse, finance, or lend the S.L.A.A. name to any related facility or outside enterprise, lest problems of money, property, and prestige divert us from our primary purpose" (Tradition 6) and "Every S.L.A.A. group ought to be fully self-supporting, declining outside contributions" (Tradition 7). Since there was no functioning institutional committee with our local SLAA Intergroup, which would have started a meeting in a treatment setting and provided weekly leadership, we had to find a way to have a meeting without violating the traditions. Fortunately, we had three volunteers among our client and staff group who got the meeting going.

The meeting is completely independent of the rest of the program. We simply provide a space for people to meet. The meeting is open to anyone who wishes to attend both from the earlier groups and outside the groups. We have no requirements for group therapy members to attend the meetings. Attendance is entirely up to them. We have the expectation that as their recovery progresses, they will establish an ongoing support system that will include relapse prevention strategies such as attendance at SLAA meetings. We do not expect therapy to last a lifetime, but recovery from the life-threatening disease of sex and love addiction will require a lifetime of awareness and caution. We assume that group members attend meetings—and it is fairly easy to detect if they do, because they tend to talk about them in their therapy sessions—but we expect them to take responsibility for this themselves. If the SLAA meeting at the end of the evening suits their needs and schedules, they attend it. If it does not, they are on their own to find other meetings that are better for them, for whatever reasons.

The three elements of our evening program for sex and love addicts—psychoeducational sessions, group psychotherapy, and a Twelve Step meeting—work well together. Each represents an important element in the recovery process. Each part works in a different way to help sex and love addicts learn to face themselves and the reality of the role of sex and love in their current lives. The parts reinforce each other and tend to complement each other as the evening unfolds. For example, certain issues may be stirred up for a person during a lecture, and he or she is then able to follow through with the issue both in the group and in a meeting. Each experience will give the issue a different slant and differing meanings. Rather than having one way to look at it or to cope, the person will be exposed to at least three different coping styles and opportunities—education, therapy, and meetings. Recovering sex and love addicts learn to integrate these various ways of responding to their needs, impulses, and coping styles. While all of these are available to the addict outside of the program, having them all together can provide a much more varied and intensive therapeutic experience.

CHAPTER 3

A Diagnostic Proposal
with Neurochemical Underpinnings

William Lord

Sexually transmitted disease rates are continuing to rise in the United States (Centers for Disease Control, 1989). A dramatic illustration is the number of reported cases of early syphilis in Philadelphia, which increased 551% from 1985 through 1989 (Centers for Disease Control, 1991). The practice of safe sex, to avoid transmission of the AIDS virus, is declining (DeBuodo et al., 1990; Centers for Disease Control, 1990; Handsfield & Schwebke, 1990). Sexually related exposés and arrests are increasingly making local and national headlines. A flourishing pornography business, estimated at over $8 billion (Attorney General's Commission on Pornography, 1986), is spreading into every community. Phone sex is readily available even to young children through 900 numbers. Attendance at Twelve Step groups such as Sex and Love Addicts Anonymous (SLAA), Sex Addicts Anonymous (SAA), and Sexaholics Anonymous (SA) is steadily growing. SLAA meetings in the United States grew from 445 in 1989 to over 900 in 1991, SAA increased from 150 meetings to 378 in the same period, and SA reported a similar growth.

Unfortunately, the medical profession continues to debate the diagnostic terminology to be applied to individuals who are powerless over their sexual and love pursuits and, consequently, find their lives unmanageable. Various labels are applied to this disorder: "compulsive sexual behavior" and "sexual addiction" are used interchangeably by Carnes (1983), Qualand (1985), and Schwartz and Brasted (1985). Coleman (1990) prefers to call these problems of "sexual compulsion." Oxford (1978) uses the term "hypersexuality"; and Barth and Kinder (1987) have made their case for "atypical impulse control disorder." The descriptions of these authors suggest that all are discussing the same pattern of behavior. Other writers find that the elements of this sexual compulsivity exhibit many of the features of a chemical dependency.

DEFINITION OF ADDICTION

The term "addiction," some suggest, should be applied only to substance abuse and dependence, on the premise that a patient can be addicted only to an exogenous psychoactive substance. There may be an increasing tenacity, by some, to hold on to such a tenet as we now see in an expanded use of the term "addiction." "No longer is addiction viewed as a single state, defined only by the presence of withdrawal syndrome, but as existing in various degrees and involving a host of behavioral, inherited and environmental factors," stated Dr. Jerome H. Jaffe, at a meeting on addiction of the Association for Research in Neuro and Mental Disease. However, Blume (1991) commented: "We may do a disservice to society by overstretching the concept of addiction. If everything is an addiction, then nothing is an addiction and we trivialize the pain of our patient."

Various activities such as eating, gambling, and sex may evolve into compulsive behaviors similar to the diagnostic criteria for the psychoactive substance dependence found in the American Psychiatric Association's *Diagnostic and Statistical Manual of Mental Disorders* (*DSM III-R*):

1. Substance often taken in larger amounts or over a longer period than the person intended;
2. Persistent desire or one or more unsuccessful efforts to cut down or control substance use;
3. A great deal of time spent in activities necessary to get the substance, taking the substance, or recovering from its effects;
4. Frequent intoxication or withdrawal symptoms when expected to fulfill major role obligations at work, school, or home or when substance use is physically hazardous;
5. Important social, occupational, or recreational activities given up or reduced because of substance use;
6. Continued substance use despite knowledge of having a persistent or recurrent social, psychological, or physical problem that is caused or exacerbated by the use of the substance;

7. Marked tolerance; need for markedly increased amounts of the substance in order to achieve intoxication or desired effect, or markedly diminished effect with continued use of the same amount;

8. Characteristic withdrawal symptoms; and

9. Substance often taken to relieve or avoid withdrawal symptoms. (American Psychiatric Association, 1980, pp. 167–68)

DSM III-R is a guide to diagnosis at a specific moment in time. There are continuing revisions of this book, and *DSM IV* is in process. The evolution of this manual is evident; in 1980 the *DSM III* did not include cocaine dependency as a diagnosis, but it was included in the Revised *DSM III* in 1987. So it may well be that today sexual addiction is, as far as the *DSM* is concerned, where cocaine was in 1980. In fact, the American Medical Association recognized alcoholism as a disease only in 1956 (reaffirmed in 1980). Some 17 years earlier, an editorial in the *Journal of the American Medical Association* ridiculed the disease concept of alcoholism and stated that the then fledgling group known as Alcoholics Anonymous was a group of "religious zealots."

Since various compulsive and addictive activities, such as overeating or compulsive sexuality, seem to fall through the cracks of standard definitions, there are two possible remedies: (1) to redefine the term "addiction" or (2) to conduct research to define addiction more clearly. Time and research in neurochemistry may necessitate the first change. The current definition already has some gray areas. For example, cannabis and other hallucinogenic drugs may produce severe impairment but are devoid of the specific signs of tolerance and withdrawal. Nicotine dependence and caffeine dependence also do not fully satisfy the criteria. A more liberal definition of "addiction" is already in use by the general public. Finding the area(s) that may cause problems and confusion and, through research, more clearly defining addiction may resolve the current dilemma. By determining what specific aspects of the term "sexual addiction" do not satisfy the *DSM III-R* criteria for dependency and then further clarifying these deficiencies so that they meet the specific requirements will result in a diagnostic category for these painful problems.

DEFINING BEHAVIORAL ADDICTIONS

There is increasing evidence to substantiate the interrelationship between psychoactive substance abuse, dependence, and behavioral addictions. For instance, as many as 70 percent of cocaine addicts entering treatment may be dually addicted to cocaine and sex such that "undiagnosed and untreated compulsive sexuality is one of the most common relapse factors in cocaine treatment today" (Washton, 1989, p. 11). From 60 to 80 percent of those addicted to psychoactive chemicals who attempt abstinence, fail within six months (Cummings et al., 1980). It is common for alcoholics and drug dependents who become abstinent (sober from alcohol and drugs) to drink larger quantities of coffee (caffeine dependence) and smoke more (nicotine dependence). Is it possible that behavioral addictions or compulsive mood-altering activities lead to relationship problems, treatment failures, high-risk sexual activity, suicide, or relapses to other mood-altering chemicals?

Addiction researchers seem to be developing new theoretical orientations (Lesieur et al., 1986) that attempt to bridge the gaps among addictions. Miller (1980) discusses four types of interconnections among problem drinking, drug abuse, obesity, and cigarette smoking: (1) there seems to be a significant correlation among unhealthy habits in general with combined health risks; (2) the use or abuse of one substance frequently serves to trigger the use or abuse of another substance; (3) addictions have reciprocity—a change in the pattern of use of one substance frequently results in a change in use of another substance; and (4) there are similar theoretical understandings for much of the behavior engaged in by addicts. Several such commonalities have been developed, including similarities in relapse patterns (Cummings et al., 1980) and pharmacology (Milkman & Sunderwirth, 1988).

According to Milkman and Sunderwirth (1983), compulsive behavior addictions are "arousal" modes of gratification that probably have effects on neurotransmitters similar to those of amphetamines and cocaine. Dependence on depressant drugs produces a decrease in neurotransmitter activity. Other researchers have hypothesized that individual differences in autonomic/cortical arousability may be a determining factor in the genesis of pathological gambling (Anderson & Brown, 1984), which is a behavioral addiction. Examining this idea, Blaszczynski et al. (1986) found differences in baseline rates of B-endorphin levels in horse race addicts compared with poker machine addicts and controls. Roy and colleagues (1986) found increased levels of norepinephrine metabolites in the cerebrospinal fluid and elevated norepinephrine in the urine of compulsive gamblers compared with normals. Along another line, Carlton and Goldstein (1986) found deficits in hemispheric differentiation in pathological gamblers similar to those found among children diagnosed as having attention deficit disorder. The results of these researchers, while not definitive, suggest a neurological substrate for this compulsive behavior.

The ultimate goal of this chapter is to promulgate a hypothetical explanation that will enable the nonsubstance-dependence problems, the behavioral addictions, to satisfy the current *DSM III-R* criteria for substance dependence. These activities, at compulsive addictive levels, have been destructive to many people. They produce problems of shame and guilt along with anxiety and depression (Carlton & Goldstein, 1986) that may be medicated by alcohol, illegal drugs, or physicians' prescription pharmaceuticals—not infrequently producing an iatrogenically induced drug dependence. To accept the constellation of symptoms and to establish diagnostic criteria will aid in destigmatizing sexual acting out and allow people to seek treatment, as happened when alcoholism was accepted as a disease and not a moral issue. By defining our terms and diagnoses and communicating in the same language, we will enable sensible research and treatment to progress in an orderly and scientific manner.

HYPOTHETICAL EXPLANATION OF BEHAVIORAL ADDICTION

Addictive and compulsive problems have been accepted, by many at least, as holistic diseases. This can be likened to an equilateral triangle in which the sides are the physical, emotional, and spiritual (willingness) aspects (see Figure 3.1). If, for some reason, one of these qualities gets out of balance, the whole triangle loses its composition. Typically, most of the therapy and treatment of sexual and other addictions has centered on the emotional and spiritual aspects. Most Twelve Step programs, and rehabilitation and other treatment facilities, focus on emotional and spiritual issues. The physical aspects of these illnesses, other than for acute detoxification, have not entered into the therapeutics except in the case of patients diagnosed with dual disorders, e.g., depression and addiction.

Figure 3.1
Holistic Disease Model

The involvement of the medical community in treatment was, and still is to some degree, limited by the mistrust of the Twelve Step programs' philosophical attitudes and by the physicians' feelings of inadequacy and/or inability to accept a role in diagnosis and treatment. For instance, until recently physicians did not know much about the neurobiochemistry of the brain and, consequently, about addictions. Therefore, most treatment dealt with behavior modification.

ADDICTION AS SELF-MEDICATION

Addictive or compulsive behavior is a response to pain and is like a pebble thrown into a pond. The initial action produces rippling waves of response and reaction. Some inciting stimulus will produce physical or emotional pain that expands progressively into the person's entire life. A system of reaction and response develops. A stimulus leading to pain will lead to suffering, which in turn evolves into pain-relieving behaviors (see Figure 3.2). In any addictive process, the stimulus that triggers the cascade may be loneliness, physical pain, low self-esteem, guilt, shame, depression, physical or sexual abuse, or other emotional, social, or physical deprivation. The consequence is the development of some reactive pain behavior.

Each individual finds some way to ameliorate whatever pain is experienced, whether it is physical or emotional. There are varying degrees of tolerance of and sensitivity to pain. The addict appears to have higher sensitivity and lower pain tolerance. The more sensitive a person is and

Figure 3.2
Pain Behavior Model

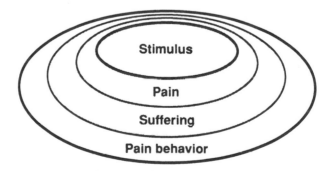

What we see is pain behavior

the less tolerant of pain, the more that person may need to find an aggressive remedy. Some people will depend on pharmaceuticals or drugs, whether they are prescription or illegal. Others will find compulsive behaviors like sexual acting out.

relief

Sex addicts early on, probably even before puberty, find there are ways in which they can reduce anxiety and tension, and enable themselves to feel more comfortable. The response to acute pain is anxiety and tension. The response to chronic pain is depression. Sex addicts will find what is going to make them feel better or, more correctly, less bad. They put on the "bandage" that they believe they need. The "bandage" or self-medication may be masturbation, viewing pornography, voyeurism and/or exhibitionism, or whatever sexual acting out they have found gives an aroused, euphoric state. For a brief moment, they leave behind a painful, lonely existence and are transformed by their acting out.

NEUROCHEMISTRY OF ADDICTION

The body, specifically the brain, has a finite number of responses to an infinite number of stimuli. The brain is made up of cells that are composed of water, chemicals, and electrical charges. They create the person. The brain clearly regulates the neuroendocrine system (Kreiger & Hughes, 1980) and is itself an end organ for neuroendocrine regulation (McEwen, 1980) by many internal and external factors (Giller et al., 1986) (see Figure 3.3). The internal factors are becoming more clearly defined, particularly in chemical abuse.

Chemical abuse may be related directly to other behavioral addictions. The psychoneuropharmacologists have discovered receptor sites in the brain to which various chemical mediators may attach. There are such receptors as opioid receptors, benzodiazepine receptors, dopamine receptors, GABA receptors, nicotine receptors, and many others. Over 50 such brain receptors have been identified. When various chemicals attach to these receptors, certain specific biological or psychological effects occur.

These receptors and mediators evolved in the human brain for specific endogenous purposes. In other words, there is something in the body that has been responsive and responds at these sites for the development and survival of the organism. In addition, frank endocrinopathies with persistent abnormal hormone levels, such as hypothyroidism, hyperthyroidism, or hypercortisolism, can often manifest psychiatric symptoms (Giller et al., 1986). These chemicals and receptor areas were not teleologically developed with the idea that man would ultimately discover exogenous substances which would produce artificial alterations. The opiate receptors

Figure 3.3
Homeostasis: Internal and External

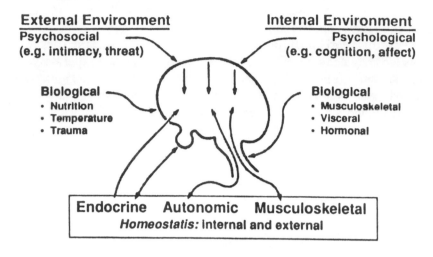

were not placed in the brain with the idea that someday man would discover morphine or heroin to alter their function, or that Valium would be developed to react at the benzodiazepine receptors.

It has been known for many years, through animal and human experimentation, that stimulation of the brain at the various centers or production of certain lesions of the midbrain, hypothalamus, thalamus, or neocortex (particularly the locus coeruleus) may cause emotional as well as physiological responses, including shame, rage, eating disorders, compulsive sexual activity, and loss of various survival activities.

DRUG OF CHOICE

All animals instinctively tend to reduce or eliminate pain. Human beings act instinctively; they also have an intellect and a conscience, and they try to gain a feeling of normality. That is, they try to feel physically and emotionally comfortable or what they would perceive as normal. If they experience pain, they find a behavioral activity or substance that minimizes the suffering. This is the "drug of choice" concept. It is an example of how people will seek a specific drug or activity to normalize their neurobiochemistry and make them feel better.

It may be easier to grasp this concept when we refer to exogenous materials that can be taken into the body in various ways: by oral ingestion, vaporization and smoking, or injection through the skin or body orifices. These compounds can be prescription pharmaceuticals or illegal drugs.

ACTIVITY OF CHOICE

Behaviors, either licit or illicit, constructive or destructive, can assist in regulating neurochemistry. Activities may change how we feel. Many are aware of the "runner's high" that is the result of stimulating the body's endorphin and endocrine systems, thereby producing an opioid effect in the brain—that is, increased endorphins—leading to a feeling of euphoria and higher self-esteem. Many people find activities and exercise that make them "feel good." The activity stimulates the endorphin system, and neurobiochemical changes occur that are perceived as pleasurable (see Figure 3.4).

Figure 3.4
Endorphin Availability

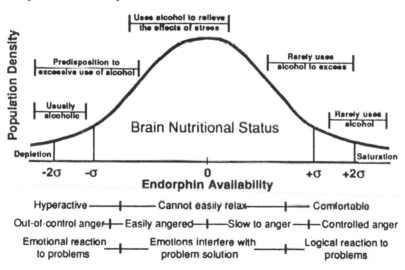

NEUROCHEMISTRY OF SEX ADDICTION

In sexual addiction, as in gambling (see Roy et al., 1986), excessive spending, or other compulsive activity, a change like that described above may occur. Individuals find that "bandage" which helps them feel better or at least not so bad. The catecholamine hypothesis of depression (now over 25 years old) stated that depression results from a relative deficit of norepinephrine in brain areas involved in the regulation of mood and affect (Bunney, 1965; Schildkraut, 1965). The serotonin system is also known to be involved in the production of depression. Anxiety and panic attacks may be explained by the increase of norepinephrine levels in individuals who experience them (Charney, 1990).

Similar systems are noted for opioid compounds through the encephalon system and for alcohol through the GABA system. In chronic alcoholics, enkephalins, including the methenkephalins, are severely depleted. Endogenous enkephalins subjectively raise the level of the feeling of well-being in the patient and increase the individual's ability to fight pain (Smith, 1986).

Scientific evidence accumulated since the mid-1970s, backed by extensive animal studies and a growing body of clinical data, indicates that addiction to alcohol, drugs, and other abusable substances is a deficiency disease involving the neurotransmitters and neuromodulators.

In the normal physiology of reward, neurotransmitters and neuromodulators work together to produce a feeling of well-being. In some individuals, however, the reward systems malfunction and the individual turns to a psychoactive substance or behavior for relief (Blum & Trachtenberg, 1987; Blum, 1977). Blum (1977) described this as the "reward cascade."

RECOVERY: CHANGING NEUROCHEMISTRY

In recovery, behavioral therapy may help change the neurobiochemical systems. Such therapy may cause changes and reduction in the sexual acting-out activity. Craving, shame, and guilt will be lessened, and this could prevent a full-blown relapse. In the recovery process, it is not what you feel or think, but what you do, that is important. If you do not do that which continues to cause neurobiochemical distress, then what you are feeling and thinking will ultimately improve and the despair, guilt, and shame will diminish. This is, in reality, the essence of the Twelve Step program. In other words, if you desensitize the neuroendocrine biochemical systems so they can return to some degree of normality, improvement will occur.

Can the sexual addict fit into this model? Is sex and love addiction a neurochemically mediated disease? The human body and brain constitutes an assemblage of chemicals and can react only in a limited and specific way. Carnes's (1983) work demonstrates that sex addicts grow up in an environment of significant dysfunction which may be passed from generation to generation. This suggests the possibility of a genetic predisposition or an inherited factor. Whether the dysfunction is genetic or environmentally induced, these are families in which there is constant stress, such as addicted parents and/or physical, emotional, and/or sexual abuse. These people live with chronic stress. They are constantly in a war zone. They try to survive and to find that "bandage" which will help them cope with the pain. This is characteristic of posttraumatic stress disorder (PTSD). Research suggests that PTSD has a unique biological profile (Visdin, 1990) consisting of alterations in the sympathetic arousal, the neuroendocrine system, and the sleep/dream cycle. This profile distinguishes PTSD from both major depression and panic disorders. The body is in a perpetual state of "fight or flight" that causes many neurobiochemical changes. Stress leads to increased ACTH levels, as well as increased levels of norepinephrine, epinephrin, serotonin, and other chemicals, which are physiological components of stress. These levels can be measured in the blood, urine, and cerebrospinal fluid.

Endorphins have properties identical to narcotic opioids such as morphine, heroin, methadone, and meperidine. Human beings (and other mammals) are under the influence of their endogenous opiates and endorphins. These cause euphoria and control anxiety, rage, and aggression (Verebey, 1983). Cocaine and amphetamines work similarly but through a different avenue, the dopamine pathway (Dackis & Gold, 1985). A deficiency in endorphins or dopamine will produce the opposite effect of the opioids: anxiety, supersensitivity to rage, aggression, depression, paranoia, low self-esteem, and suicidal ideations (see Figure 3.5).

Figure 3.5
Psychological Effects of Opiate Agonists

Endorphins ≅ Opiate Agonists
⇩
Psychological effects of opiate agonists
tranquilization, anti-depressant, anti-rage,
anti-aggression, anti-paranoia, decrease of suicidal ideation,
increased self-image
⇩
Psychological function
⇩
Psychological homeostasis

Similar
withdr.

The typical withdrawal syndromes of opiate or cocaine addicts and of sexual addicts are extremely similar and follow the patterns mentioned above. The original work by Jellinek in alcoholism produced what is known as the Jellinek chart of alcoholism (Jellinek, 1960). This demonstrates the gradual but continued downward spiraling course into the abyss of addiction, with increasing loss of control and continuing restrictions of all areas of the addict's life, to the eventual end of death, mental institution, jail, or recovery. Only with abstinence and recovery will the addict climb out of the depths of despair and hopelessness to a fuller, more rewarding life. This same paradigm can be adapted to cocaine addiction as well as other substance and behavior addictions, including sex and love addiction.

TOLERANCE AND WITHDRAWAL IN SEX ADDICTION

Chronic stress, like chronic drug use, leads to the dysfunction of neurotransmitter systems such as the endorphins (Verebey, 1983), dopamine, opioid peptides, tetrahydroisoquinolines, serotonin, and others. Such an imbalance in these reward systems can be related to genetic neurotransmitter system problems, hormone abnormalities, immune system alterations, chronic drug abuse (Blum & Trachtenberg, 1987), nutritional imbalances, or other causes as yet undiscovered. Another component of this imbalance may be that the biosynthesis of these neurotransmitters is slower or inactive, or the enzymatic degeneration is too rapid. Another possibility is that sufficient neurotransmitter concentration is present in the brain but for some unknown reason the release mechanism is defective.

The net effect is to reduce the neurotransmitters at the synapse of the cells. This deficiency will produce anxiety, supersensitivity to rage, aggression, depression, low self-esteem, and suicidal ideations. This is a neurobiochemical response and effect. The sex and love addict may try to remedy this defect by increasing sexual or romantic acting out in order to increase the amount of neurotransmitters (as the drug addict does by ingesting more drugs). This floods the system with endogenously produced endorphins or some other neurotransmitter, which increases the synaptic transmission. A short-term response of "well-being" occurs and, as the neurotransmitter is quickly depleted, leads to a state of despair, distress, and increased craving. With continued use, there is further interference with the release of the neurotransmitter and blocking of the receptor sites in the reward areas of the brain. At the same time, the number of receptor sites may increase, resulting in an even greater discrepancy between the amount of transmitters available and the number of receptor sites occupied.

The neurotransmitters are now in short supply and more activity is needed to obtain a "high." This is the essence of "tolerance." Because the defect may occur in the part of the brain that functions to maintain life, the alcohol, drug, or activity may be perceived as being required for life. As such, the behavior acts as a basic drive that is compulsive, just as drinking water when thirsty or eating food when hungry are required to sustain life. This craving remains at a high level, and the individual experiences a generalized feeling of depression and unhappiness, ultimately followed by the "crash," characterized by intense craving, anxiety, insomnia, restlessness, and anhedonia. Therefore, the individual will continually, despite all adverse effects, try to regain that "high" or attempt to achieve a feeling of normality. Addiction is acquired like a habit but, once acquired, continues as a nonextinguishable response. Rather than being eliminated, an addiction is a chronic disease that is managed like diabetes.

I do not mean to imply that someday a "silver bullet" will be found that will be a sudden cure for addiction. Insulin, which is a chemically active hormone in the body, has not yet cured all the ills of the diabetic patient. Antibiotics have not solved all the problems of the patient who contracts syphilis or pneumonia. Sexual addiction, like all compulsive addictive dependencies, is a multifactorial disease. It is a disease of physical, emotional, spiritual, behavioral, financial, and social problems. It will require more than a pill or potion to repair the damage.

Much investigation still needs to be done. More research is required to evaluate the neurobiochemistry of the sex addict and compare it with that of normal controls, as well as of those with other addictive problems, including drug-abusing patients. Criteria to differentiate sexual addiction from other primary psychiatric diseases need to be established. Work needs to be done to find those markers which may be particular or peculiar to the sexual addict (if there are any).

It is quite conceivable that with the understanding of brain chemistry in addiction, there may come a time when neurochemical assessments are performed on patients as they come through the door for treatment. This evaluation could put patients into different classes or subclasses calling for particular kinds of treatment. The neurotransmitter assays may lead to some specific pharmacological intervention in therapy. Neuroactive chemicals or pharmaceuticals are becoming very specific. Clomipramine

(Anafranil), for example, seems to have a particular and specific place in the pharmacological treatment for obsessive/compulsive disorders.

The Twelve Step programs seem to help in normalizing the neuro-biochemistry. This, of course, is only speculation, since there are no scientific studies in this area. Such an idea is at present impossible to test in people. However, sexual abstinence with caring, loving help and the observed experiences of others seems to make the acute withdrawal phase less painful or, at least, more tolerable. The feeling of safety gained from sponsors, Twelve Step meetings, and other members of the program, as well as in group and individual therapy, should help to reduce the chronic stresses these patients experience in dealing with people and life. Over-coming the paralyzing fear of sharing in meetings, with sponsors and other members of the program, helps to remove or reduce the stress of secrecy, with a resulting decrease in the "fight or flight" neuroendocrine challenge. The recovery process is a desensitization to fear and risk taking. People in a state of meditation or prayer and who accept a Higher Power (God), seem to have profoundly different neurobiochemical events going on in their brains than people who are actively involved in addiction, who are hyperactive and have abnormal levels of various hormones, such as adrenaline, as well as other neurotransmitters, coursing through their systems.

Organizing a treatment regimen around an assessment of brain function will not alter the dependence on a spiritual element in recovery that is a basic tenet of all Twelve Step recovery programs. The neuroendocrine biochemical system is the only way the body can respond, with cellular molecular electrical changes, and this itself is a creation of a Higher Power.

SEX AND LOVE ADDICTION AND PARAPHILIA

Sex and love addiction does not fit into any of the present diagnostic categories. Placing it in the category of paraphilias does not seem adequate because the description in *DSM III-R* is not comprehensive enough. As we have argued, sex and love addiction has all the symptoms of dependence: (1) persistence despite adverse side effects, (2) increasing tolerance, and (3) a specific withdrawal syndrome. The paraphilias, as described in *DSM III-R*, have no such symptoms outlined. Even with the worst-case scenario of paraphilias, the *DSM III-R* (1987) states: "Criteria for severity of manifestations of a specific paraphilia; Severe: The person has repeatedly acted out of the paraphiliac urge" (p. 281). There is no mention of the elements of compulsivity, tolerance, or withdrawal that are seen in sex addiction patients.

MASTURBATION

There is no classification in the *Diagnostic Manual* for compulsive masturbation. This activity, especially when done compulsively, may be physically harmful and cause severe emotional distress. Masturbation may frequently cause the person to be late for work, skip work entirely, or miss other activities—these are among the criteria noted in the *DSM III-R* for "dependence." Masturbation also keeps alive a persistent and distressing fantasy life. Fantasy may preoccupy the sex addict to the point of his or her being ineffectual in work or play—for instance, constantly "cruising" tennis courts, gyms, golf courses, theaters, or restaurants. This fantasy life, as the disease progresses, may become increasingly destructive and vicious, and can ultimately lead to sadism, masochism, and even homicidal or suicidal ideation.

RESPONSIBILITY

Some may have the concern that the label "sex and love addiction" will be used to excuse all varieties of behaviors and to get offenders "off the hook" legally and personally. Without a specific definition and criteria for the diagnosis, this may happen. There are articles and books in which the authors use their own subjective definition for this condition. The philandering husband who has casual or frequent affairs may invoke the defense of sexual addiction and yet not have any addictive element in his activity—compulsive, perhaps, but not addictive. Schneider, in her book *Back from Betrayal* (1988), defines an addiction as "a self destructive relationship with a mood altering drug or behavior. To be addicted to a behavior is to continue that behavior even though it has negative consequences. In sex addictions, what defines the addiction is not the number of sexual encounters, but rather the compulsive nature of the behavior despite the cost. Every addiction has two critical elements—a behavior disorder, and a thinking disorder which denies and rationalizes the addictive behavior" (Schneider, 1988, p. 225). There needs to be more involved in addiction than loss of control: diarrhea, for example, is a function demonstrating a loss of control, but it is not an addiction. Carnes (1983) likewise seems to have a simplistic definition of addiction as a "pathological relationship." The use of the term "addiction" in such a casual and nonspecific, nonscientific fashion may result in having the concept invoked to excuse aberrant behavior. Although an addict may not be responsible for causing the disease, certainly the addict needs to be held accountable for his or her actions, especially after proper diagnosis.

CONCLUSION

Addictions must have three basic elements: (1) a compulsion to continue, despite adverse consequences; (2) increasing tolerance—the need to use or do more to achieve the same effect; and (3) a definite withdrawal phenomenon. If these apply to any specific chemical or behavior, the syndrome should be labeled an addiction.

Anyone who has experienced a sex addiction can vividly describe these three elements: compulsion, tolerance, and withdrawal. None of the authors who have written about sexual addiction has denied the existence of the compulsive element. So, in this area, they are all correct but not complete; the areas of tolerance and withdrawal are defined by these authors. A characteristic withdrawal occurs when the sexual activity is discontinued. Without the stimulus (continued sexual acting-out behaviors that produce high levels of neurotransmitters in the brain) withdrawal will occur and produce anxiety, supersensitivity to rage, aggression, depression, agitation, confusion, insecurity, and possibly suicidal ideations. This is a neurochemical response and effect. The withdrawal experience is documented and described in *Sex and Love Addicts Anonymous* (Augustine Fellowship, 1986). Withdrawal may be an extremely painful process, both physically and emotionally, and can even lead the addict to the point of suicide. At times, it may be necessary to hospitalize individuals who are in withdrawal until they can be mentally stabilized.

There are other areas of activity, such as compulsive "cruising" or compulsive "intrigue," that do not fit into the *DSM III-R* and yet are an integral part of the sexual addict's behavior. This needs to be rectified.

The lack of definition of the disease of sexual addiction leaves a void in the lexicon of diagnoses. Subsequently, the lack of identification and treatment of many suffering people persists. As the controversy over diagnosis rages, lives, reputations, families, careers, and relationships are being destroyed.

The basic elements of an addiction process are very much a part of a true sex and love addict's life. A hypothetical explanation utilizing the possible neurobiochemical basis for addictive disease has been proposed. Care must be taken that we do not profess to know more than we do regarding the connections of substance abuse and behavior problems, so as not to give the impression that this is any more than a theory. As with many diagnoses in medicine, and more particularly in mental and emotional disorders, we have no definite test or marker to validate our clinical impressions. We establish certain criteria, and through our judgment of patients' symptomatology we put them into some category of diagnosis.

Concl.

We then can use what we subjectively think is the best available therapy in an effort to produce a change—to improve the quality of life for that individual and all those who care about him or her, and to improve society.

I propose that behavior addiction be added to the *Diagnostic Manual,* using all the parameters for substance dependence but replacing "substance" by a specific behavior—sex, gambling, or eating. An additional requirement would be that the individual be free of any substance abuse, dependence, and/or addiction for a minimum period of time—as little as 3 months but preferably 6 to 12 months. An evaluation of all exogenous chemicals for any possible neurotropic effects is also needed.

REFERENCES

American Psychiatric Association (1987). *Diagnostic and Statistical Manual of Mental Disorders*, 3rd ed., rev. Washington, DC: APA.

Anderson, G., & Brown, R. (1984). "Real and Laboratory Gambling: Sensation Seeking and Arousal." *British Journal of Psychology* 75:401–410.

Attorney General's Commission on Pornography. (1986). *The Final Report.* Washington, DC: U.S. Department of Justice.

The Augustine Fellowship, Sex and Love Addicts Anonymous. (1986). *Sex and Love Addicts Anonymous*. Boston: Fellowship Wide Service.

Barth, R. J., & Kinder, B. N. (1987). "The Mislabeling of Sexual Impulsivity." *Journal of Sex and Marital Therapy* 13:15–23.

Blaszczynski, A. P., Winter, S. W., & McConaghy, N. (1986). "Plasma Endorphin Levels in Pathological Gambling." *Journal of Gambling Behavior* 2:3–14.

Blum, K. (1977). *Alcohol and Opiates: Neurochemical and Behavioral Mechanisms*. New York: Academic Press.

Blum, K., & Trachtenberg, M. (1987). "Addict May Lack Some Neurotransmitters." *U.S. Journal of Drug and Alcohol Dependence* (July):15.

Blume, Sheila. (1991). Personal communication. (March 29).

Bunney, W. E., Jr. (1965). "Norepinephrine in Depressive Reactions: A Review." *Archives of General Psychiatry* 13:481–494.

Carlton, P., & Goldstein, L. (1986). "Physiological Determinants of Pathological Gambling." In *A Handbook of Pathological Gambling*, ed. T. Galski. Springfield, IL: Charles V. Thomas.

Carnes, P. (1983). *Out of the Shadows: Understanding Sexual Addiction*. Minneapolis: CompCare.

Centers for Disease Control. (1989). "Summary of Notifiable Diseases U.S. 1988." *Morbidity and Mortality Weekly Review* 37, no. 54 (Oct. 6):20–38.

———. "Heterosexual Behaviors and Factors That Influence Condom Use Among Patients Attending a Sexually Transmitted Disease Clinic—San Francisco." *Morbidity and Mortality Weekly Review* 39, no. 39 (Oct. 5):685.

———. "Alternative Case Finding Methods in a Crack-Related Syphilis Epidemic—Philadelphia." *Morbidity and Mortality Weekly Review* 40, no. 5 (Feb. 8):77.

Charney, D. (1990). "The Neurobiology of Anxiety: Neurodevelopmental Hypotheses." *Psychiatry Letter* 7, no. 6 (July):1–5.

Coleman, E. (1990). "The Obsessive Compulsive Model for Describing Compulsive Sexual Behavior." *American Journal of Preventive Psychiatry and Neurology* 2, no. 3 (May):9–13.

Cummings, C., Gordon, J. R., & Marlatt, G. A. (1980). *Relapse Prevention and Production: The Addictive Behaviors.* Oxford: Pergamon Press.

Dackis, C., & Gold, M. (1985). "Bromocriptine Treatment of Cocaine Addiction." *Psychiatry Letter* 3, no. 8 (Aug.):45–50.

DeBuodo, B., Zinner, S., Daanen, M., & McCormack, W. (1990). "Sexual Behavior of College Women in 1957, 1986, and 1989." *New England Journal of Medicine* 322, no. 12 (Mar. 22):821–825.

Giller, Earl, Mason, J., Kosten, T., Frank, J., Ostroff, R., & Harkness, L. "Psychoendocrine Assessment of Diagnosis and Suicidality." *Psychiatric Letter* 4, no. 3:13–18.

Handsfield, H. H., & Schwebke, J. R. (1990). "Trends in Sexually Transmitted Disease in Homosexually Active Men in King County, Washington, 1980–1990." *Sexually Transmitted Diseases* 17:211.

Jellinek, E. M. (1960). "The Disease Concept of Alcoholism." *Canadian Medical Association Journal* 83:1341.

Kreiger, P. J., & Hughes, J. C., eds. (1980). *Neuroendocrinology.* Sunderland, MA: Sinauer Associates.

Lesieur, H., Blume, S., & Zuppa, R. (1986). "Alcoholism, Drug Abuse, and Gambling." *Alcoholism: Clinical and Experimental Research* 10:33–38.

McEwen, B. S. (1980). *IN: Neuroendocrinology.* Sunderland, MA: Sinauer Associates.

Milkman, H., & Sunderworth, S. (1983). "The Chemistry of Craving." *Psychology Today* 17:36–44.

Miller, P. M. (1980). "Theoretical and Practical Issues in Substance Abuse Assessment and Treatment." In *The Addictive Behaviors.* Oxford: Pergamon Press.

Oxford, J. (1978). "Hypersexuality: Implications for a Theory of Dependence." *British Journal of Addiction* 72:299–310.

Qualand, M. C. (1985). "Compulsive Sexual Behavior: Definition of a Problem and an Approach to Treatment." *Journal of Sex and Marital Therapy* 11:121–132.

Roy, A., Adinoff, B., Roehrich, L., Lamparski, D., Custer, R., Lorenz, V., Barbaccia, M., Costa, E., & Linnoila, M. (1986). "Pathological Gambling: A Psychobiological Study." *Archives of General Psychiatry* 45:369–375.

Schildkraut, J. J. (1965). "The Catecholamine Hypothesis of Affective Disorders—A Review of Supporting Evidence." *American Journal of Psychiatry* 122:509–522.

Schneider, J. P. (1988). *Back from Betrayal.* Minneapolis: Hazelden Foundation.

Schwartz, M. F., & Brasted, W. S. (1985). "Sexual Addiction." *Medical Aspects of Human Sexuality* 19:103–107.

Smith, David. (1986). "Decreasing Drug Hunger." *Professional Counselor* (Nov./Dec.):6.

Verebey, K. (1983). "Endorphins and Human Behavior." *Psychiatry Letter* 1, no. 5 (May):1–5.

Visdin, G. (1990). "Post Traumatic Stress Disorder." *Psychiatry Letter* 7, no. 3 (Feb.):1–5.

Washton, A. (1989). "Cocaine May Trigger Sexual Compulsion." *U.S. Journal of Drug and Alcohol Dependence* 13, no. 6 (June):11.

CHAPTER 4

Using Individual and Group Therapy in Recovery

Eric Griffin-Shelley and Helen Griffin-Shelley

Outpatient therapy of sex and love addictions involves a variety of components including individual and group psychotherapy, psycho-education and bibliotherapy, and self-help work. After initial diagnostic formulations have been made by the therapist and the patient, a treatment plan is needed to guide their work. A key element in this plan is the role of individual and group psychotherapy. In this chapter, we will address the value of each of these therapeutic approaches, with special emphasis on the potential for healing the sex and love addict. Then we will examine the different ways that these two therapies can be used alone or in combination. Finally, we will discuss some of our failures as indicators of the limitations of our therapeutic endeavors.

Many of our initial contacts with clients are initiated because of a crisis or extremely stressful event in the sex and love addict's life. Someone, something, or some event has compelled the person to seek help. For one client, it was a confrontation with the police over sexual acting out in exhibitionistic ways. For another, a spouse had threatened him with divorce if he did not do something about his "sexual problem." A woman felt near the verge of suicide because her sexual behaviors seemed out of her conscious control and likely to cause her to violate her most sacred beliefs and commitments. Another client sought help because she found that she could not break away from a drug-addicted boyfriend who was becoming more paranoid, jealous, and physically dangerous.

All of these clients came to us for help, and most of them wanted to be "fixed" immediately. One characteristic of addicted people is that they are used to a "quick fix," and they often lack the coping skills to tolerate delays in gratification or to take their time in building a successful recovery program. They want to be better now! It is important to respond to the sex and love addict's need for immediate attention, but this does not mean that treatment planning will not require careful thought and possibly frequent revision.

For example, we recently consulted with a man in his forties who was referred by his wife's outpatient therapist. He had a history of cross-dressing and had difficulty functioning in normal sexual relations. His wife was becoming intolerant of his sexual deviance and his lack of attention to her sexual needs. As she became more assertive, he decided that he needed to be evaluated. He was studying to become a counselor after a career in education, which he indicated was part of his motivation for seeking treatment. He did not want his own sexual problems or sexual issues interfering with his work with his clients.

This man had a number of experiences in therapy previously and had been in both individual and group treatment. He had sought therapy for gender-identity issues, but he indicated that he had not made much progress with this approach and wanted to examine the value of an addictions approach to his compulsive need to dress in women's clothing and to masturbate while holding women's underwear. He reported that he had gotten to the point in his gender identity therapy where others were experimenting with living as the opposite sex—men would dress in women's clothing to test how they would feel being related to in public as women. He could not take this step, nor could he seriously consider medication or surgery to change his gender identity.

After talking with him for a while, we wanted to see how easy it would be for him to consider the idea of living without masturbating for a time. In the Sex and Love Addicts Anonymous (SLAA) program, the goal for sexual sobriety is to have sexual contact in the context of a committed relationship. He was married, and he and his partner seemed committed to their relationship. We wanted to see if he could imagine going without satisfying his sexual needs in isolation (masturbating alone). He found this idea almost impossible to grasp, so we suggested that there were addictive qualities to his intense dependency on masturbation. We encouraged him to try an addictions approach since his work with gender identity had not achieved the results that he desired. His treatment plan included initial psychoeducational efforts, such as reading relevant literature and attending at least six SLAA meetings. After this beginning step, referral to individual or group therapy (or both) would be appropriate, depending on his response to the initial phase of therapy.

INDIVIDUAL PSYCHOTHERAPY

Individual therapeutic treatment of sex and love addiction has many advantages. The first, and perhaps most obvious, is that the one-to-one contact in the session provides the person with undivided attention. Many of our clients can feel jealous of others in a group or angry that they do not get enough time or attention. In individual therapy, there is no one else to compete with the person for the time or attention of the therapist. Many of our clients come from family environments where they were neglected or abused. Parental relationships were poor or destructive, and often sibling and peer relations were not much better. Their capacity for meaningful interpersonal relationships and intimacy has been severely compromised by their early developmental experiences. Their sex and love addictions have further damaged their ability to have a close, nonsexual contact with another human being. This essential skill needs to be nurtured and developed in the one-to-one contact of individual therapy.

The second advantage and goal of individual work is to help the sex and love addict experience the unconditional acceptance and love of a primary relationship. In this context, the sex and love addict can learn to trust and to begin to open up to the world and relationships that previously had seemed so dangerous and complicated. In terms of Eriksonian stages, the first stage of development is basic trust. Because of the family environments described above, the sex and love addict often has not had another person with whom he or she could feel close, loved, and accepted. One client of ours, who dreamed of being a policeman as a child, had a father who was cold, aloof, and distant. His mother was passive and insecure, and tended to gossip with neighbors. He never felt that his parents took his side on anything, especially when outsiders like teachers were involved. He was always seen as guilty by his parents. He grew up longing for unconditional love and found himself driven to compulsive affairs. He preferred women "who could not say 'no' to me" because it gave him that sense of total acceptance which he so lacked in his childhood. In his recovery, unconditional acceptance by his therapist has been a crucial part of his individual therapy.

A third benefit of individual therapy is the opportunity to reduce shame and to confront defenses. Sex and love addicts tend to come from families that are rigid about rules and distant in terms of expressing emotions. They can use shaming and guilt-inducing responses to control behaviors. Many clients come to treatment with an intense burden of shame that has them convinced they are bad, worthless people. A client came into treatment after remembering some incestuous contacts with his mother that left him feeling terribly embarrassed, ashamed, and guilty. His mother had never had a good relationship with her husband and turned to her son to meet her emotional needs. This imbalance in their relationship led to many intrusive and controlling behaviors on her part, including bathing her son when he was eight or nine, with special attention to cleaning his genitals. His protests were dismissed because of her own unmet needs. However, the nature of the relationship and his mother's insistence on her altruistic motives left him filled with a heavy burden of shame. His individual work helps him to untangle this complex web of feelings.

As people begin to open up and take a more honest and deeper look at themselves, they encounter defenses that they have erected to keep them safe on their life's journey. Confronting defenses is a frightening and difficult task, and requires a lot of trust and support. In the context of individual sessions, sex and love addicts can begin the process of examining and dismantling the defensive systems that they have built up over the years. Letting down the walls requires trust and safety. Sometimes sex and love addicts find this first in their Twelve Step meetings, where other addicts are sharing their most inner feelings and experiences in recovery. Others find safety and openness in their group therapy sessions. Some need the protection of the one-to-one therapeutic relationship, where they can be sure of acceptance and continuity of care in order to take an honest look at how they fool themselves and the rest of the world.

A fourth advantage and goal of individual treatment is to reduce the sex and love addict's character defects and to identify concurrent addictions. Addictions seem to foster certain character traits that may or may not have been present prior to the activation of the addictive process. Addicts typically are narcissistic, self-centered, and grandiose. Some have called addicts "his or her majesty the baby," because of the childlike demands of addicts for immediate gratification and the supremacy of their own needs over the needs of others. Often, sex and love addicts are not confronted about these character traits by others in their self-help program. Sometimes therapists may hesitate to be direct about "negative" personality characteristics of group members. Individual therapy may be the only opportunity for the recovering person to get feedback about dysfunctional personality traits.

One sex and love addict had terrible personal hygiene, which reflected his inability to care for himself and his low self-esteem. He was rather idiosyncratic and isolated, so there were few people in his world who would tell him how he looked. At meetings, he came and went without comment. His group was afraid of his fragility and his anger, so they held back from telling him about this defect of character. The job fell to his individual therapist, who could address this issue in the context of a relationship where concern and trust were already established.

Individual work can also identify and begin to deal with other addictions, such as compulsive overwork, overeating, exercise dependence, religiosity or driven confessions, power problems, or issues with money. Many compulsive/addictive people struggle with many compulsive behaviors. One client had made great headway with his sex and love addiction, and was starting to build some genuine self-esteem. In the safety of his individual work, we were able to address his overeating. He had gained over 60 pounds in his initial recovery from his sex and love addiction. He could not tolerate feedback about his "switching addictions" from others, but he was able to look at his behavior with the support of his individual therapist. Although he was afraid to bring up his eating in his therapy group, he had established a pattern of dealing with things first in his individual work and thereby gaining the courage to share with his group.

It is often the task of individual psychotherapy to address dual or multiple diagnoses. In our general approach to addictions, we look at establishing a pattern of sobriety before delving into other issues. Sometimes, however, other problems are contributing to continued acting out. Depression, anxiety, and trauma and tragedy in current or past life can make sobriety from sex and love addictions seem almost impossible to achieve. A young man with whom we were working ran from treatment rather than face his many compulsive behaviors. He appeared to be simply narcissistic and "not ready" to change, but after a week on an antidepressant medication, he began to open up as he never had before. Another addict complained of fears, paranoia, and tightening in his throat that made him feel like he would not be able to breathe, especially when he was in group therapy. When his panic attacks and anxiety were dealt with, he was more able to concentrate on his addiction recovery.

Post-traumatic stress disorder, victimization, and revictimization are issues that many sex and love addicts need to deal with in order to have healthy self-esteem and adequate coping skills. If possible, we try to postpone work on these types of issues during the first year of recovery. However, there are times when this is not possible because the trauma experiences are triggers for continued acting out in sex and love addictions. A woman in her forties was unable to resist sexually acting out, even though part of her wished to be nonsexually intimate, because she felt that she had to satisfy the needs of her male partner who had been kind and gentle, and had agreed to hold her and talk to her when she was in need. The roots of this behavior are in her incestuous relationship with her father, whose sexual needs she was called on to fulfill when her alcoholic mother was not available. She became suicidal because of this dissociative split in her personality and required hospitalization in order to establish an understanding of the effects of her childhood trauma on her current behavior and addiction recovery process. She needed to work out these issues in individual therapy because the shame and guilt that she felt were too great to allow her to disclose her history in her group.

In sex and love addiction recovery, then, individual psychotherapy has many important goals and advantages. The sex and love addict has the undivided attention of the therapist. In this one-to-one relationship, trust and openness can be experienced, perhaps for the first time in the person's life. Issues like shame, guilt, and defensiveness can be addressed in a safe, supportive environment that is not always present in a group, where a number of other people may act out their own issues with the person. Character defects and concurrent addictions can be examined as the recovery process progresses. Other mental health problems like depression, anxiety, and trauma can be tackled, especially when they are undermining serious efforts at recovery by the sex and love addict.

GROUP PSYCHOTHERAPY

In addition to or sometimes instead of individual psychotherapy, group psychotherapy can contribute to the recovery from sex and love addiction in a number of important and different ways. In a group setting, the crucial coping mechanism of learning to be open and honest can be observed and practiced. In our groups, we stress the importance of this first goal of therapy by beginning the group sessions with a statement that includes the phrase "honesty is the key to sobriety." Since secrecy and shame drive addictions, especially sex and love addictions, change occurs when an individual decides to become truly open, honest, and vulnerable.

Sex and love addicts often can create the illusion of openness and sensitivity by sharing and getting others to talk about sexual and romantic relations and experiences. Usually, however, the sex and love addict is doing this to find ways to manipulate and seduce others. For example, sexual talk, sexual jokes, seductive glances, exhibitionistic clothing, and subtle touches are often carefully designed to "feel out" the openness of the other person to some sort of acting out. In the SLAA program, these behaviors are called "intriguing" and "cruising," and are ways of finding sexual and romantic partners for addictive acting out rather than the intimacy that they seem to be creating.

In recovery, group therapy can be especially helpful in breaking down this facade of pseudo intimacy because other group members are quite sensitive to the phoniness of these behaviors. In fact, in one recent group session, the members gently confronted one person's tendency to give caring responses to others and to give up his time to talk so that others would have more time. They experienced his pseudo caring as a way of avoiding self-disclosure and openness. He was creating barriers to intimacy and closeness in the guise of caring and attentive behaviors toward others. The group members really wanted to get to know him, and needed him to be more honest and open with them about his real thoughts and feelings about his own life, not his reactions to the lives of others. This was a skill that he had not yet mastered because of his great fear of acceptance and the fantasy that others would reject him if they really knew what he was like inside.

Skill building, for example, becoming honest, is a learning process that requires understanding, observation, modeling, and practice. For most sex and love addicts, there has never been a safe environment in which to acquire this coping skill. Their families were rigid, closed, secretive, and detached, or they were chaotic, intrusive, confusing, and enmeshed. Peer relationships tended to follow similar patterns, and they frequently tried to skip over the developmental task of learning intimacy with peers and jumped into primary relationships. In other words, they switched their unmet dependency needs from family to a particular peer and did not learn how to be independent and open with others who were equals. In group therapy, they have the opportunity to discover how to be open and honest with equals.

A second significant advantage of group therapy is that it offers the sex and love addict a safe place to get honest feedback from peers. In Twelve Step meetings like SLAA, there is a rule against "cross talk." What this means is that when someone shares in a meeting, no one else in the meeting can respond to what that person says in terms of giving their own thoughts, reactions, or advice. A person in the meeting can share something about themselves and their own recovery based on what another shares, but the second sharing cannot be in the form of corrections, rebuttals, or reinforcement of the first person's sharing. For example, if one person shares that he or she thought that his or her sex and love addiction was caused by sexual abuse in the past, no one else should get up and say that person is all wrong or all right. Other persons can share their own experiences and thoughts about the cause or origin of their own sex- and love-addicted behaviors, but they should not be trying to change what another person has shared. These boundaries are important in Twelve Step meetings because they are not group therapy sessions.

Group therapy sessions provide consistency in membership and a time frame that allows for feedback, reactions, comments, advice, and interpretations between group members. One reason for this is that the members of the group are committed to be there each week and the membership is limited. In SLAA meetings or other Twelve Step fellowships, there is no requirement for membership other than the desire to stop a pattern of compulsive sex- and love-addicted behaviors. Attendance is not taken, and the makeup and size of the meeting can vary from week to week. Group therapy sessions are paid for and require a group leader. In fellowship meetings, contributions are voluntary, as is the leadership. Members chair meetings, but their commitment is usually for one month at a time. In group therapy, the group leader is a paid professional who makes a commitment to be available to the group members each week at the same time on an ongoing basis.

These features enable group sessions to provide opportunities that are not available to the person who attends only Twelve Step fellowship meetings. Members can use their therapy groups for accountability and reality checks that may or may not be available to them elsewhere. For example, a person who joins a group for therapy makes a commitment to attend the sessions regularly, and the other group members will hold the member accountable if there are absences or problems with lateness. A sex and love addict who is a salesman found the accountability to attend therapy a surprising and at times difficult benefit. He was quite independent both at work and at home, so no one in his life ever asked him to be accountable for his time or noticed (or at least told him if they did notice) when he was irresponsible about his commitments and the needs of others (such as the need of group members to have him be there when he indicated that he would be). This slipperiness about accountability was an important aspect of his sex and love addiction because he would take advantage of his freedom to act out sexually and did not have to be concerned that others would ask where he was or what he was doing. He got in the habit of not thinking how others might feel about his absences and lateness. His group therapy, then, was a chance to start to learn that accountability is part of openness and honesty, and that these will lead to the real intimacy that he was longing for rather than the pseudo intimacy that he created while acting out.

Feedback from peers also provides the sex and love addict with a "reality check." Recently, a sex and love addict told us that he needed to get some feedback from his group about whether he was "blowing smoke up my ass" (his term for being dishonest with himself). He was having trouble keeping to his commitment to be involved in only one relationship at a time. He realized early in his recovery process that he was good at convincing himself it was okay to do things that were really not in his best interests. His addiction to compulsive, multiple affairs had clearly convinced him of his ability to "con" himself. He used his group members as a reality test because he knew that they cared enough about him not to tell him things they thought were untrue, even if the feedback was painful to him.

This may sound like something that most people would normally get from their peers. Most sex and love addicts do not have a peer group with whom they are open and honest. This is the next advantage of group therapy. It allows sex and love addicts to have a safe peer group with whom they can share the intimate details of their lives, their deepest thoughts and feelings, and learn to experience the caring and support that such a group can provide. Sex and love addicts do not know how to have normal relationships. Their families had poor and even damaging relationships with them while they were growing up. They usually started acting out their sex and love addiction between the ages of 6 and 12. Consequently, they had secrets to keep from their adolescent peers and never learned to really be open and honest with equals. They tended to jump over peer relations and tried to have intimate or at least sexual contact with another who would make them feel loved and accepted. However, these relationships tended to be pseudo intimate—if that—because the addict was not really capable of real intimacy.

Before becoming intimate with an equal or dealing with the harm of early life relationships, most sex and love addicts need to learn how to have normal relationships with equals. Some accomplish this in their Twelve Step meetings. Others need the higher level of structure and support offered by group therapy. One sex and love addict we worked with found it easy to talk with others and at times was quite annoying because he did not know when to stop talking. In fact, his tendency to talk in such a narcissistic way alienated others rather than bringing them closer. He tended to intellectualize and philosophize—traits that he was aware of— and drove others away—even to hating him and his lack of proper control, boundaries, and social appropriateness. After extensive group psychotherapy, he broke down and cried one day about his fears of abandonment that were rooted in his adoption experience. This revelation would not have seemed possible without the support and normative experience of his group therapy.

As with individual work, group therapy offers an opportunity for cathartic emotional experiences, such as the one described above, that need to happen in a larger interpersonal environment than a one-to-one session. Sometimes our group leaders will structure this work in terms of a role-playing situation, a gestalt experiment, or a psychodramatic session. At other times, the safety and support of the group are enough for someone to share a traumatic life experience. In one session, a sex and love addict began to focus on his detachment and inability to concentrate. Rather quickly, he plunged into a flashback of being sexually abused as a child, a memory that he had previously repressed. His group therapy was a safer place to experience this forgotten experience because his one-to-one sessions too closely resembled the abuse situation.

This leads us to another advantage of group therapy: the chance to experience nonsexual intimacy. Individual psychotherapy is obviously suited to the development of closeness and trust, but with people who have been abused and violated in such relationships, as is the case with incest and sexual abuse survivors, the group may in fact be a safer place to begin to learn how to be intimate. Our groups are separated by sex with the purpose of reducing the threat of finding a sexual partner in the group. Obviously, this does not help with homosexually oriented clients, but since our referrals come from both heterosexual and homosexual orientations, separating by sex provides the best chance for reducing the number of potential sexual partners in the group.

Sex and love addicts need a place where they can learn how to talk about their innermost needs and feelings. Intimacy is letting go of all barriers and allowing another person to know who you really are. It is letting go of your masks, defenses, and images. It is "letting your hair down" and "letting it all hang out." Some people can do this with only one person at a time and are too threatened by a group situation to reveal themselves as they truly are. For others, one-on-one contact is too much; they need the safety from abuse and manipulation provided by the group context. Seductive or harmful feedback or reactions by some group members will be pointed out by other group members or the group leader, so the group member is less likely to reenact the abusive experiences of the past. In individual work, there is the possibility that the therapist and the client will develop a "mutual admiration society." In the group, this incestlike dynamic will be less likely to occur and should be challenged by the rest of the group if it does develop.

One client of ours placed us on a pedestal and projected the need for an all-knowing, all-powerful parent onto the individual therapist. With the aid of the group process, this idealization was able to be addressed and the dynamic changed in a way that offered the sex and love addict sources of nurturing and support besides the individual therapist. This is a common part of individual work and is usually referred to as transference. This example was of a positive transference, but the group can also help recovering people deal with issues of negative transference, where the person feels that the individual therapist is somehow harmful or is being destructive or manipulative. Again, the reality check function of the group can assist the person in learning how to have nonsexual, intimate relationships with others.

The last helpful aspect of group therapy that we will cover is universality. This does not mean that there are not other goals and advantages of group therapy; it simply reflects the main aspects of this approach to treatment that we have identified. "Universality" refers to the experience that people have when they realize they are not alone in terms of having difficulty with sexuality and romantic relationships. One of the most powerful aspects of group therapy and Twelve Step programs, and their related literature and publicity, is that people who are suffering with the disease finally discover that they are not the only person who is hurting because of sex and love. Addictions tend to isolate people, and sex and love addicts tend to be extremely isolated even when their acting out may involve many other people.

We frequently have the experience of sex and love addicts telling us that they feel so relieved, so comforted when they find out there are others who have the same affliction. Most have agonized in silence and secrecy, and feel that a great weight has been lifted from them when they experience the universality of going to a Twelve Step meeting or a group therapy session where they hear other sex and love addicts talking about the same struggles, the same shame, the same low self-esteem that they have been tortured with for many years. Often, they have felt subhuman, like perverts or outcasts. They are well aware of the highly judgmental and moralistic attitudes in our society toward people who cannot control their sexual or romantic relationships.

Often they have been called "whore," "slut," "pervert," "deviant," "nymphomaniac," or "stud." Even if others have not explicitly said things like this to them, they have called themselves these and other names. This type of name-calling is very damaging to the already low self-worth of sex and love addicts. Name-calling implies that the people who are called names are in control and that they have a choice about how they think and behave. Addicts in active addictions are not in control and do not have the range of choices that normal individuals would have. Sex and love addicts are sick, and their illness drives them to act in ways that violate their own as well as society's norms, expectations, values, and laws. Consequently, addicts are outlaws to themselves and feel as if they do not fit in, nor are they acceptable to society. Unfortunately, rather than setting limits on addictive behavior, this tends to drive sex and love addicts deeper into their addiction because they are desperately trying to find love and acceptance in their acting out. When they come to a group or meeting and find love and acceptance for simply showing up, the healing process is initiated. When they hear that others have the same problems and difficulties with impulse control, thoughts, feelings, and behaviors, they start to feel that they are once again part of the human race and to experience the universality of mankind.

Group therapy, then, has a number of goals and advantages vis-à-vis individual psychotherapy. In group psychotherapy, sex and love addicts can learn to be honest, open, and real, an essential coping skill for healthy, authentic living. Group therapy can provide feedback, "cross talk," reality checks, accountability, and consistency. The sex and love addict can begin to learn how to have normal relationships, especially with peers. They can discover how to get and accept support. The group can be a safe place for cathartic emotional experiences. The sex and love addict can learn and practice nonsexual intimacy, and can experience universality that breaks down the perception of being all alone. Some of these benefits of group therapy can also exist in individual work, such as feedback or nonsexual intimacy, but the quality and quantity will be different. Often it is helpful to have both, and to share group experiences with the individual therapist and vice versa.

INTEGRATING INDIVIDUAL AND GROUP WORK

In our experience, sex and love addicts have taken many paths to recovery. Some involve therapy; some do not. The following cases illustrate some of the therapeutic journeys that we have shared with recovering sex and love addicts. In our minds, the ideal recovery would include both individual and group psychotherapy with an intensive Twelve Step recovery program using meetings, sponsors, and tools of recovery like prayer and writing. Of course, reality does not follow the lofty images of our fantasy, and each person's recovery follows a process that is often at least somewhat unpredictable. Our hope is that these stories will help addiction professionals to support sex and love addicts in their growth toward health and healing by teaching them that they need to be open and flexible in their approach. Too often in the past, addictionologists have seen only one way to the truth, and at times have abused clients who are not willing to "surrender" and do things their way. While "letting go and letting God (or Higher Power)" is important in freeing oneself from the grips of an addiction, this does not mean elevating one's counselor or others into the role of gods who know everything. Some therapists volunteer for this lofty, all-knowing role, endangering themselves and their clients in the process.

Individual Psychotherapy First, Group Therapy Later

Our first case is the story of a clergyman in his mid-forties. He did not volunteer for treatment but was referred after his assistant discovered a room full of pornography and reported it to the authorities. He felt terrible shame and guilt over the referral process but also had had the intention to change his addictive habits for a long time. He felt paranoid about being discovered because he not only purchased pornography (to which he compulsively masturbated) but also visited adult bookstores and public bathrooms where he would act out with anonymous sex. He dreaded possible scandal and publicity if his behaviors were to come to light. He hated himself for violating his own moral and religious codes, and was furious with himself for not being able to stop even though he had tried on many occasions. He was afraid that his acting out with others would lead to contracting AIDS and subsequent death. He felt trapped, with no way out.

After three initial assessment sessions, he agreed to undergo a therapy process in order to establish sobriety with his sex and love addiction. When we discussed the various elements of a potential treatment plan, such as individual and/or group psychotherapy, bibliotherapy, and attendance at SLAA meetings, he was able to consider only reading and individual work. He felt too ashamed to attend SLAA meetings and was too uncomfortable to attend group. He felt safest in a one-to-one setting with someone whom he had begun to trust. He could not tolerate the idea of having to share his story with anyone else.

During the first six months of his treatment, he experienced moderate success. He was able to throw out his pornography collection and did not purchase any more (both "bottom lines" in his recovery program). He was able to attend therapy regularly and had begun to learn to open up and be honest about his experience. He was still quite detached and isolated. He could not share his inner pain with anyone other than his therapist, and he continued to act out occasionally with anonymous sex and compulsive masturbation. His self-worth had begun to improve, but he was still excessively paranoid about public exposure. He imagined that people knew more about his problem than they really did, and feared that they would contact the local newspaper. Mainly because of his continued "slips" (breaking his "bottom line" promises to himself that he would not engage in these behaviors that he had defined as addictive for him), we began to discuss other tools of recovery that would help to move him further along the path that he wanted to follow.

We both agreed that an obvious addition to his initial program would be attendance at Twelve Step meetings and/or group psychotherapy. He chose to try group therapy because the group was smaller and would include the same people each time. Again his barrier to helping himself was his profound sense of shame. His shame grew out of a family that was quite distant and detached. They were also quite religious, and he felt terribly sinful in his actions. His father was sick most of his life and did not pay much attention to him. His mother was nice to him but preoccupied with her husband. His older brother tried to play a paternal role, but his direction mainly came in the form of anger and shaming criticisms. Our client grew up expecting little attention from others, and what he got was frightening and felt awful. He tended to avoid being singled out in his personal life, yet he chose a profession that required him to be the leader of his congregation.

This split between a personal life that he kept hidden and repressed and a professional life that put him in a public and helping role continued in his active addiction and in the initial stages of his recovery. Integrating his public life and his private life happened more readily in meetings and/or group therapy. He had a great fear of being discovered. He expected others to find him bad and unworthy, much as his older brother had so many years before. Even though he knew he would find relief in the universality of the problem that he would experience from attending group, he could not volunteer to expose himself to potential anger and criticism.

Finally, he decided that he would have to push himself despite his anxiety, and he began to attend group therapy. His progress was slow at first. It was months before he could reveal his profession to the group, even though by then most had probably figured it out. He took months to be able to talk to the group about problems that he was having with his assistant or thoughts that he was having about his brother. With each step in self-disclosure came an increase in self-confidence and an improvement in his recovery program. Almost without noticing it, he ended acting out in anonymous sexual contacts at bookstores or bathrooms. He began to feel less paranoid and more peaceful. He stated that he finally was beginning to "feel like a man instead of a little kid." The power of the group process was healing in many ways.

Group Psychotherapy First, Individual Therapy Later

The second case example is a sex and love addict who started his treatment in group therapy and took a long time before he was ready to consider individual treatment. He is in his late thirties and works for the government in a procurement job. He was married but divorced after four years. He is chemically dependent and attended Alcoholics Anonymous (AA) for five years before coming to the SLAA program. When he first interviewed with us, he asked to be in a group only. His acting out involved compulsive masturbation, the purchase and use of pornography, and anonymous sex in bookstores. He attended SLAA meetings but did not have a sponsor. He had established "bottom line" behaviors and thought that a group therapy situation would help him to reinforce what he already knew about his recovery process. He also had a tendency to be isolated, and he thought that the group might also help him with this as well.

He was extremely frightened of dealing with any of his childhood issues. As many abuse victims do, he tended to make his childhood abuse unreal and to blame himself for everything. His father was a teacher who had a terrible temper (only at home). He had been absent when our client was young and was physically abusive when he reentered the home. His relationship with our client was distant and shaming. He would say things like "I don't know what to do with you; go talk to your mother." His mother would react in a similar way, and our client was left feeling like he didn't belong anywhere.

Our client had great difficulty with his relationships. He described having a period of "years" during which he was a virtual "recluse" living in his parents' home and drinking alcoholically. He reported that he "always" destroyed the relationships that were closest and that he valued the most. He "drove away" his wife with verbal abuse and "the silent treatment." He ended relationships with friends and AA sponsors with angry fights and hostile withdrawals. He could not tolerate the idea of getting an SLAA sponsor. Yet he wanted to be in group therapy because individual therapy was much too threatening and dangerous to him.

As his therapy progressed, he was more and more able to identify himself as a victim of physical and emotional abuse at the hands of his parents and his older brother. He became increasingly aware of his own vulnerability in relationships and the ways that his intense sensitivity could lead to sexual acting out. For example, one evening at an SLAA meeting he wanted to talk with another person. However, the person ignored him and was talking to someone else. He went to an adult bookstore on his way home and started a binge that lasted for four days and almost cost him his job because he did not call in. Later, he could say that he was so hurt by the rejection that he needed to self-medicate, to nurture himself in the only way that he knew how: acting out sexually.

Only after a year of group therapy and a recovery program that still was not producing sobriety for more than a few weeks at a time did he consider engaging in individual psychotherapy. He was extremely frightened at first and had many boundary issues that threatened to end the therapy relationship. For example, we had difficulty finding a day and a time. Late afternoon appointments were hard because the traffic was unpredictable. He came late a few times and expected that he could have his full session anyway. He felt hurt and abused by the normal limits set around therapy sessions, and wanted his therapist to give him special treatment so that he could feel cared about and safe. He could hardly tolerate the discussion of expectations and needed a great deal of support and feedback from friends in the program who were in therapy and had the same sort of limits. He was terrified of being seduced into trusting and then being beaten for making a mistake, as he had been in his family.

After a lengthy process of testing and coming closer, then pulling away, he was finally able to commit himself to individual psychotherapy. He struggled to find a safe place, and as he grew more comfortable, he was able to reveal how extensive the damage was to his personality. More in-depth psychotherapy revealed a dissociative disorder that had developed out of the abuse that he had experienced as a child. He finally was able to remember that his sixth grade teacher had indicated that he had "two different personalities." He could be warm, friendly, adventuresome, and caring sometimes. At other times, usually when his addiction had been triggered, he was cold, hostile, aloof, and abusive. The one side was like a hurt child who needed nurturing, and the other side was like a caricature of his abusive father. Once these sides were clarified, the integrative work could finally be done. For this client, this latter work could happen only in the context of individual psychotherapy, which in turn could happen only after a positive experience with group therapy.

Individual Psychotherapy Only

Our third case is an example of a sex and love addict who needed only individual psychotherapy. She came to us with a history of bulimia that she had overcome with the help of individual psychotherapy. She already had decided that this type of help was what she needed, and did not really consider Twelve Step meetings or group therapy at the time we developed her treatment plan. She acted out in terms of romantic attachments that were not satisfying but could not be ended. She had had a series of boyfriends who left her feeling unlovable, alone, and unable to find a permanent partner. She tended to give in to the demands of her partners and not to make any demands of her own. She felt worthless and lost.

She was confused by her relationship with her father, who seemed distant and rejecting but who also took care of her financially. She did not hold a job and make her own way in the world. She spent two hours every morning getting ready to go out. She spent hours every weekend meticulously cleaning her sports car. She did not have women friends and was quite isolated. Her social skills were poor, as was her self-esteem. She had not developed a career and was looking for a mate to take care of her.

She had trouble committing to the therapy process despite her experience of success in the past. She preferred to meet every other week and would cancel a session if her parents did not give her the money to pay for it. At one point, she met another sex and love addict at a gym and abandoned her treatment in favor of a relationship with him. She rationalized to herself that "maybe two sex addicts can find happiness together." The inevitable failure of the relationship finally came, and she returned to her individual psychotherapy with increased enthusiasm. As we often do to evaluate the level of resolve to change, we suggested that she try attending some women's SLAA meetings. She quickly became involved in the meetings and the program, and soon announced that she had a sponsor. Her recovery began to progress dramatically at this point as she began to use the support of the meetings and her therapy to begin to take charge of her life.

She made a commitment to herself to stay out of relationships for at least six months. Initially she could not imagine doing this, but as the time passed, she discovered that she was beginning to like herself for the first time in her life. She was developing a female support system and was looking for other ways to become more assertive and independent. After about a year, she decided that she wanted to try her wings without therapy for a time. She was reassured that it would be all right for her to check in, or come back for more individual work, or simply live her life as it was becoming. She chose the latter without any need for a group therapy experience.

Another sex and love addict came for individual psychotherapy after he had established sobriety with his sex and love addiction. He had gotten sober from alcoholism with AA and used the same principles with his sexual acting out, which involved serial affairs with men that left him feeling hollow and empty. He also had noted tendencies toward overeating and overworking in his character. He could overspend and overpray as well. He had a handle on his compulsive behaviors but wanted to understand the deeper driving forces behind them.

He felt ignored, abandoned, and used by his parents. He felt like a stranger in his own house. He often spent hours and hours on sophisticated intellectual pursuits that his parents never seemed to understand. He felt used by them to take care of his younger siblings. At times, his father had a violent temper, and was harsh and judgmental of our client's abilities. He had grown up looking for a father figure in teachers and other older men in his life. He had discovered sexuality as a teenager and used masturbation to soothe and nurture himself in an environment that was cold and rejecting. He also discovered that he could feel close to other boys and men by being sexual with them, and mistook sexual contact for intimacy. This confusion lasted for years, throughout his painful addiction to sex. He was finally able to obtain abstinence from compulsive masturbation and sexually acting out with others outside a committed relationship.

He was having some trouble at work with his temper, and this was the motivating factor for coming for individual psychotherapy. He had lost his temper with some of his students and was afraid of repercussions from the school administration or the parents. He was aware that his explosive anger was related to unresolved issues from his family of origin, especially his deep feelings of hurt and abandonment by his father. He was trying to be a good father to his students, and became enraged when they were not able to respond to his kindness and efforts to reach them. He was able to use the structure and support of individual sessions to focus on these issues, to identify and talk through his feelings, and to do some gestalt exercises that enabled him to work through his blocks around communicating with his father. His therapy was relatively short-term, and the idea of group psychotherapy was never an important part of the treatment plan. Both he and the preceding case made good use of their individual work and developed a strong support system in the fellowship of SLAA. They did not need to take advantage of the group therapy process in their recovery from sex and love addiction.

Group Psychotherapy Only

We also have individuals in sex and love addiction recovery who are involved only in group psychotherapy. As outlined above, there may be important psychodynamic reasons why some clients need or prefer group therapy. For others, the reason can be purely financial. Individual psychotherapy tends to be expensive even when medical insurance pays for part of the cost.

One sex and love addict came to us with severely impaired social skills. He had had a long and frightening history of prior psychotherapy that included periods in a state hospital. He had been divorced and lost custody of his children during this period in his life. He had been addicted to drugs and was left partially brain damaged and disabled as a result of his excesses. He was estranged from his current wife and worried excessively about the well-being of their young son. He acted out with compulsive masturbation, going to "go-go" bars and observing women dancing almost nude, and getting into masochistic encounters with women behind screens in bookstores.

When he joined the group, his self-care and grooming were quite poor. He tended to talk almost autistically, without much sense that anyone else was present. He attended SLAA meetings but tended to be overly intellectual, without any concrete results. When he was initially given feedback in the group sessions, he had very little tolerance for what others were saying to him. He tended to become so enraged and defensive that group members ceased to interact with him. He was narcissistic and grandiose when he presented himself, and other people tended to respond to him with anger or neglect.

During the almost two years that he has been in his group, he has made remarkable changes in a number of areas. He is taking better care of himself in terms of grooming, hygiene, and overall health. He has been able to establish some bottom-line behaviors that he can adhere to in his recovery. He can ask for and accept feedback from others. He is starting to develop a support system. He is able to look more realistically at his marriage and the potential for its restoration. He has been able to keep contact with his son, which did not happen with his other children. He has become more focused, warmer, and more gentle in his interactions with others. He has been able to use the group for accountability and reality checks. He has been able to be consistent in his attendance and has remained committed to the group process.

Another sex and love addict came to us asking for group psychotherapy after he had been dumped by the one woman he had ever really loved. He had fallen into a deep depression at the loss of this relationship and sought help through SLAA on the advice of some of his friends in AA. He had become extremely isolated and could not function in terms of day-to-day responsibilities like doing the dishes or reading the mail.

This sex and love addict described a wild and abusive trail of sexual and romantic encounters that started with an incestuous relationship with his sister. She made him feel cared about "for the first time in my life," and for years to follow, he sought love and caring through sexual gratification. He became addicted to alcohol and drugs. He married a woman he did not love but who seemed to worship him and they had "great sex." Her father provided him with a job but the marriage eventually failed, and with it went his employment. He drifted from job to job and relationship to relationship. He was looking to be taken care of and was never really able to be intimate or equal with any of his partners. His self-image was horrible, rooted in the neglect and rejection that he felt from his parents, especially his father, who had been verbally abusive as well as indifferent.

He finally began a recovery process from chemicals but became entangled in a dependent relationship. This time he was dependent on the woman and felt that he had had his first "real relationship" with anyone. He could not meet her needs, and after he began to recover from the blow of her rejection, he became determined to grow in a way that would allow him to have a committed relationship with an equal partner. He had an SLAA program that involved meetings, meditation, and readings. However, his social contacts were quite poor. He was looking to learn how to have healthy relationships with both sexes in his group therapy experience.

Individual and Group Therapy Combined

Our preference, especially when a client is in crisis or needs an intensive program, is to combine individual and group psychotherapy with psycho-educational experiences like bibliotherapy and use of Twelve Step self-help, support groups like SLAA. One client came to us in a marital crisis. His wife had discovered that he was again involved in sexual relationships outside of the marriage and wanted him to receive inpatient treatment or terminate the marriage. He had begun attending Sexaholics Anonymous, but he was not involved in any therapy and had not been able to stop acting out with compulsive affairs.

He indicated that he was willing to do whatever was recommended to him because he felt he could no longer pursue his life of dishonesty and duplicity. He had had a long history of affairs starting shortly after he was married. He stated that his "biggest hits" came from having sexual encounters with married women who were "only interested in sex." He became intoxicated with the idea that he was so "special" that these women would "do anything for me." He found that he was not performing well at work due to his extensive fantasy life and his elaborate schemes to cover up his activities. He "got off on" having power over women and feeling that they could not resist him.

He came from a working-class family that seemed to feel less than others around him. His father was distant, rigid, and controlling. His mother was passive, unaffectionate, and gossipy. He had fallen in love at a young age and had been dumped when his girlfriend went away to college. He was so devastated that he vowed never to allow a woman to have that much power over him again. He felt that his parents "never took my side" with school authorities or other adults, and consequently he always felt he was doing something wrong. Eventually, he decided that he might as well do wrong things, since that seemed to be what his parents expected of him. He remembers compulsive masturbation as a teenager as well as voyeurism, looking into neighbors' bedrooms with his telescope every night.

We began treatment with an intensive combination of individual and group work along with increased reading and attendance at SLAA meetings. He understood that if this level of treatment was not sufficient, we would refer him to an inpatient program for four to six weeks. He took his recovery quite seriously and was able to establish some clear bottom-line behaviors, including no casual sex, no affairs, no phone calls discussing sex, no cards or letters to prospective sexual partners, no sexual jokes or innuendos, and no flirting, intrigue, or cruising, especially at lunchtime. Eventually he was able to add compulsive masturbation and fantasies to his bottom lines. He achieved sobriety fairly quickly with the support of the meetings and his therapy. He had some slips along the way, but he has not had a full-blown relapse.

His wife went for residential treatment of codependency, but he had decided that he needed to end the marriage in order to be able to feel good about himself. He went into the relationship "for all the wrong reasons" and had acted out his anger compulsively with betrayals of trust almost from the beginning. He took a long time to get an SLAA sponsor and continues to have a strong, positive transference to his individual therapist. He uses his group for emotional support and as a "reality check" so that he is not fooling himself about his issues and progress. He clearly benefited from the intensive outpatient program of therapy, psychoeducation, and Twelve Step support. He was able to avoid residential treatment and has made significant progress due to his dedicated and consistent work.

TREATMENT FAILURES

Our review of individual and group treatment would not be complete without an acknowledgment that this intensive approach does not always work. Examples of our treatment failures will highlight some of the dangers and pitfalls of our work. Our first case is a client we forced out of treatment due to our misjudgment about his readiness to join group psychotherapy. This professional man in his forties had begun his recovery with individual psychotherapy. He had been an overeater who was able to make excellent use of Overeaters Anonymous. He had discovered some further difficulties with compulsive masturbation, inappropriate relationships, and excessive sexual fantasies, and sought therapy for these issues.

His initial phase of treatment went quite well. He appeared to have an idealized transference with his therapist and significant difficulties with his social relationships. He was quite isolated and intellectualized, and had no social supports. He tended to overwork and had difficulties with boundaries and saying "no." We recommended that he join an outpatient group, and he agreed. However, just prior to attending the group for the first time, he called with what appeared to be a poor excuse. A confrontive approach was used in response to what seemed to be social anxiety and childish manipulation of the therapeutic relationship. Unfortunately, the depth of his fear was so great that he chose to end his therapy rather than consider attending the group session. The therapist had underestimated his anxiety level and misinterpreted his needs to the point where the client no longer felt safe, even in the individual relationship.

Another client who seemed to need a combination of individual and group therapy agreed to go along with the treatment plan, but her compliance became an obvious desire to please the individual therapist rather than a felt need of the patient. This sex and love addict had had a number of extremely dependent relationships, some of which had placed her in great physical danger. She grew up with a father who hated women and a mother who pushed her into the role of her father's caretaker. She had fantasies of replacing her mother and marrying her father. Her relationships with men tended to be abusive, neglectful ones in which she gave more than she received.

She was extremely isolated and had no close friends. She seemed to be overly dependent on her therapist and had little life outside of work, therapy, and meetings. She had no friends to call, but she found people to take care of in the meetings and elsewhere. She seemed to be an excellent candidate for the socializing experience of a therapy group. She went to the group at the suggestion of her individual therapist, but she attacked the group leader and hated the group almost from the beginning. She projected a lot of her neglect and abuse issues onto the women's group leader and often felt hurt and stirred up by the group experience. At one point, she became suicidal because she felt pushed too far, and a graceful way was found for her to leave the group. In retrospect, she went to the group for the wrong reasons: to please her therapist and to continue to be a "good girl" for an authority figure.

Another sex and love addict found the whole therapy process abusive and was especially upset by the group experience. This man in his sixties had been referred for treatment by his employer because he had taken advantage of a counseling relationship with an adult and had sexualized the encounter. After he was reported and during the evaluation process, he revealed half a dozen compulsive sexual relationships as well as visits to pornographic bookstores that made him feel terribly humiliated but that he was unable to resist. He thought that once he had been confronted, he would again institute the rigid self-controls that he had let slide, and would not need further intervention.

His treatment plan called for an intensive program of individual and group psychotherapy because of the seriousness of the boundary violation in his professional relationship. Sexualizing counseling relationships has incestuous dynamics and was quite traumatic for his victims. He went along with the plan and revealed his anger and feelings of victimization only after a long time. He never really got involved in the group process and always sat on the periphery. He talked, but rarely shared his own personal struggles. He was able to establish and maintain bottom-line behaviors regarding adult bookstores, sexual relations, and masturbation. However, he was highly resistant to looking deeper into his core issues of neglect and abandonment.

Eventually, as it became more obvious that he was attending the group but only taking up space, his treatment plan was revised to exclude the group sessions and the emphasis was placed on individual therapy. After some time, he was able to begin to share his rage and feelings of humiliation at "having" to attend the group therapy session. In fact, he did not see the need for any therapy, and felt degraded and abused by the fact that anyone expected him to need therapy at all. He was able to work with this distortion and knew that he was projecting somewhat, but he took a long time to renegotiate the relationship to a point where there was more mutuality and trust.

The final example is of a client who had an extremely intensive outpatient treatment that was not enough. This sex and love addict in his twenties engaged in exhibitionism and anonymous sexual encounters in parks, bathrooms, and rest areas. He had been able to get sober from alcohol and drugs with the help of Narcotics Anonymous. He wanted to do something about his compulsive sexual behaviors and went for inpatient treatment. He had a period of three to four months of sobriety following this treatment, during which time he was attending SLAA meetings. He started having slips and relapses, and sought out psychotherapy. He was seen individually at first but was quickly encouraged to join a group as well. Eventually he was being seen twice a week in individual sessions and once a week in group. His acting out did not stop despite this intense level of support.

He seemed to be hypersensitive to sexual triggers and was acting out on the way home from meetings and therapy. He had been sexually molested by his father and was terrified about working on this issue. His family was not at all supportive; in fact, his sister once said to him in anger, "Do you think you were the only one to be molested? Why can't you forget it and move on with your life?" He could not move on, and he could not find a safe place in the world. He could not manage to move out of his parents' home, although he did make a few abortive tries. He finally lost his job and became desperate and suicidal. He went to live in a halfway house far from home that seemed to offer the type and length of treatment that he really needed.

CONCLUSION

Treatment planning for sex and love addicts can be challenging and difficult. Most of the time, especially when they seek professional treatment, their addictions have created serious disturbances in their lives in terms of their behaviors, moods, and thoughts—as well as affecting their families and friends, their finances, and their moral and spiritual lives. They often need intensive intervention. At times residential treatment may be necessary, usually when a person is suicidal or unable to stop high-risk behaviors, but eventually the sex and love addict will need an outpatient therapy program. A large part of this plan is deciding the role of individual and group psychotherapy.

Individual therapy offers many advantages, such as the therapist's undivided attention and the privacy of a one-to-one contact. In the individual therapy relationship there is an opportunity to work on fundamental issues like trust and openness with another human being. As this relationship develops, the one-to-one therapy session becomes a safe place for sex and love addicts to work through shame, embarrassment, and their system of defenses. In addition, the individual therapist can assess the existence of other addictions or mental health problems like anxiety disorders and serious depression. Character defects can be addressed and worked on. The primary therapy relationship can be the place where the person works through profoundly damaging early traumas and posttrauma effects.

Group psychotherapy has its own unique set of goals and benefits. In group therapy, members learn to be honest with other people in general and not simply with one person. They have a chance to observe role models and to practice life-giving coping skills. The group sessions are a chance to get feedback and a reality check from people who know the cons and games of addicts. Normal, healthy relationships, especially with persons of the same sex, can be learned, and there is the opportunity to get and accept positive support. In group, there are times when members have cathartic emotional experiences that give freedom to emotions long hidden from themselves and others. The group is a place where the members can experience nonsexual intimacy and discover what this is, how it feels, and how to re-create it in their own lives. Group psychotherapy breaks down the isolation and aloneness of sex and love addicts because they experience being in a room where everyone else has the same problem that they have.

Of course, with the many advantages of both types of intervention, the best possible course would seem to be to provide each recovering sex and love addict with both. We have provided examples of how some sex and love addicts need to have individual psychotherapy before they are ready and able to join a group therapy program. Other sex and love addicts are better treated with group therapy first and individual therapy later. Some sex and love addicts seem to need only individual therapy, while others seem to do well with just group work. Many, however, seem to need the combination of individual and group work as well as attendance at Twelve Step meetings such as SLAA and bibliotherapy (readings).

We need to be clear that our work is not always successful. There are obviously many reasons for failures in psychotherapy. Some of these are due to the fact that some persons are not psychically ready to undergo treatment and recovery, and may need to suffer more before they will be able to do the hard work of getting better. Other failures are due to our limitations as treatment professionals—our own impatience, other character defects, and lack of the appropriate skills, experience, and training. Some sex and love addicts feel abused by the treatment process and cannot tolerate it. This can be because they are not at a point where they can be sufficiently open and vulnerable, or it may be because they are not coming to therapy voluntarily—they may have been sent by the courts, their lawyer, a boss, or a spouse. For some sex and love addicts, intensive outpatient treatment is not enough even when combined with short-term (four to six weeks) residential treatment. These addicts may need to live in a community of recovering people such as in a halfway house. In any case, our limitations and failures can help us to do more and better with the other sex and love addicts we encounter in our professional work.

Individual and group psychotherapy with sex and love addicts is a challenging and rewarding work. As therapists, we need to remember to keep the communication lines open between the individual and group therapists. In our program, we require monthly notes from the therapists about the progress of the sex and love addicts with whom they are working. Since many of our clients have come from homes and parents who were not able to meet their needs and may have damaged them in the process, we need to function as "good parents" and communicate openly and frequently with each other. It is especially important that we be able to tell other treatment professionals involved with a client our concerns about our own and their limitations and inconsistencies, because these may be crucial links in understanding the illness of the person we are trying to help.

CHAPTER 5

Group Process Issues
in Men's Groups

Jeffrey Kaufman

This chapter is based on my experience over the past several years conducting a weekly outpatient psychotherapy group for sexually addicted men and supervising other therapists conducting similar groups. The psychotherapy group is part of a recovery program for persons who have identified themselves as sex- and love-addicted. My approach to group therapy is rooted in psychodynamic psychotherapy and a group-as-a-whole perspective on groups. A good example of the integration of these two ways of thinking elaborated into a general theory of group psychotherapy is Ashbach and Schermer's *Object Relations, the Self and the Group* (1987).

Early in my practice I had heard that Freud said he learned the most by listening to his patients. I have placed listening to patients above all other sources of learning. This chapter owes most to the men in the sex and love addicts group. The shame, the pain, the persistent yearning for recovery, and the courage of the men in the group have infused the group process and have guided my therapeutic understanding. I have also learned about sex and love addictions from the writings of Patrick Carnes (1989) and Eric Griffin-Shelley (1991).

GROUP MEMBERSHIP AND IDENTITY

The group is specifically for men who have self-identified as sex and love addicts. Identification with and participation in a sex and love addiction Twelve Step recovery program is usually the context in which persons enter the group and is a key aspect of the group setup. It places group membership in the larger community of recovering persons having a common experience and frame of reference for self-understanding as sex and love addicts. It also establishes a common bond between members that is significant in terms of group cohesion and the supportive capacity of the group. The sense of community and membership provides a common language, a common value system, a sense of belonging, and an identification that helps to secure the recovery process for group members. It places addictive behavior and the meaning of this behavior in the protective context of the recovering community. It helps group members to be clear and honest with themselves and provides a safe harbor for recovery.

This common identity among group members fosters reorganization of identity and a sense of self. The values, mutually nurturing attitudes, and newly found friendship experiences with other men in the therapeutically secure outpatient environment of the group fosters change intersubjectively and in group members' relations with their own selves. As identity is increasingly influenced by identification in the therapeutic bond of the group, the shame-fueled cycle of addictive behavior is disrupted. The potency of core shame and worthlessness is reduced and healthy self-esteem develops. Members begin to experience themselves in the eyes of others in group (mirroring) and, using this mutual self-recognition, they begin to internalize a nurturing self-regard. This reorganization of the sense of self establishes a base for self-regulation of dysregulative acting-out tendencies of the sex- and love-addicted person. The men in the group severely lack the experience of relationships with other men. These relationships are therapeutically valuable, and the need for them is clearly expressed by group members: "I've never related to men." "Having relationships with men helps me to really look at everything differently." "My way of relating has been to sexualize, and if I didn't sexualize, there was no interest." "These relationships are what my recovery is all about for me."

RITUALS

Rituals are part of any group process. These are the unwritten rules for the repeated behaviors the group goes through at each session. They are the implicit and explicit signifiers of group membership. In the recurring ritual behavior, group members are reminded of, and joined together through, the ritual enactment. Associated with specific rituals are specific traditions and values of the group.

Our sex and love addiction groups have structured rituals for opening and closing. These group rituals have a variety of functions. They explicitly and/or implicitly affirm the context of the group within the Twelve Step community. Rituals may state rules and purposes of the group in a simple and concrete way. They also can assert the therapeutic sanctity of the time in which the group meets. They have significance in affirming and confirming membership in the therapeutic community.

Opening and closing rituals vary somewhat among the groups, but they include group recitation of a statement: "We come together as a group to be honest with ourselves and with each other. What's said in the group stays in the group. Honesty is the key to sobriety." This is followed by a ritual of "checking in" or opening statements. Each member says a few sentences to explain where he is at the start of the session. For example, Ted [not real names], a 38-year-old sex and love addict "checked in" one evening by saying that he had had a dream about being sexually molested and had experienced an up-and-down week. He wanted to talk about it during the group. Another example of "checking in" is a statement Ted made many months later. He said, "Last week in group, Larry gave us feedback that sounded just like my father. I felt he shamed me. I didn't say anything at the time, but want to talk about this tonight." Each group session ends with a "closing statement" ritual that comments on the members' experiences that evening. An example of a closing statement is "This was a good group for me tonight. I appreciate everyone's support. I want to affirm Tom for his honesty tonight. What you said, Tom, was helpful to me. This group is my lifeline."

In one group, members felt that they sometimes did not get enough time to speak. In the name of fairness, the group established a ritual of going around the circle each session with each member allotted equal time. This ritual also functioned to minimize an increased sense of closeness between members that had been longed for, yet was experienced as threatening. The ritual was developed by the group in response to an issue in the group dynamic. Rituals that emerge out of the life experience of the group serve a group dynamic function. The therapist needs to be aware of this and to articulate this for the group.

Ritualized behavior comes into play in active sex and love addictions. In recovery, we try to reverse this process by building healthy rituals to harness—in a noncompulsive way and in the service of the therapeutic aims of group—the addict's tendency to invest in powerful rituals. Ritualization is a component of the addictive cycle as articulated by Carnes (1989). According to Carnes, it emerges as an enhancement of addictive preoccupation with sex and love, and functions as a method of "preparing for sexual activity to take place." Carnes notes that it has a trance induction-like effect. In this way we may understand addictive ritual as marking the transition phase to the disassociated addictive state.

OUTSIDE-THE-GROUP CONTACT AMONG MEMBERS

It is a rule of thumb in traditional group psychotherapy to establish a rule against contact between members outside the group, in order to keep issues inside the group. In our group, we encourage the development of supportive relationships between members outside the group. Our groups are designed to accommodate the specific therapeutic needs of sex and love addicts. Therefore, the group needs to integrate the Twelve Step support group strategy of sanctioning and encouraging outside-the-group contact into the group psychotherapy arrangement. The supportive value of outside-the-group contacts for members struggling with intense acting-out urges—usually associated with deep shame-based impulsivity, loneliness, feelings of devaluation, and self-disintegrative trends—is vital to recovery from addictions. Twelve Step programs encourage, among other things, daily phone contacts with sponsors as a way to cope with daily cravings, especially during withdrawal. When someone first attends a Twelve Step meeting, it is common for "old-timers" to give newcomers their phone numbers and encourage calls to help with recovery. Recovering addicts know that in early recovery 24-hour support may be the difference between success and failure. Members often have contact with each other before and after Twelve Step meetings.

The role of the group as part of a recovery program requires that its mode of operation be consistent with the values and ways of the Twelve Step program. The group is structured to harness the therapeutic potential in the relationship between members outside the group, for instance, through supportive availability when members are experiencing "triggers" and are about to act out. Group support for feelings that trigger anger, shame, emptiness, and so on cannot be adequately provided without the availability of support outside the group. Support consists not only of members helping each other with specific pitfalls in the recovery process but also of the cultivation of friendships in the face of the chronic experience of isolation and worthlessness. Outside-the-group contact helps to validate the authenticity of caring communicated among participants in the group. It also helps with the integration into life experiences of the therapeutic understanding and norms present in group therapy.

What of clinical concern about the violation of protective boundaries and group therapeutic process? Experience has shown that while there are issues and problems which need to be managed by the group therapist, such as subgrouping, conflicts, and secrets that occur in outside-group contacts, there is no basic endangerment of the boundary security of therapeutic group process. Subgrouping (or pairing) occurs when a number of group members interact in such a way as to establish an inclusion/ exclusion boundary within the group. Members may get together socially between group sessions, may meet before or after the group to socialize or discuss recovery issues in their lives, or may have telephone contact.

This is, as described above, a valuable and essential part of a sex and love addicts' therapy group. However, since it may involve subgrouping, it presents a number of risks for the therapeutic aims that the group therapist needs to be aware of. Subgrouping may occasion scapegoating, may foster feelings of being left out, may divert group issues, or may result in or be motivated by disruptive forces in the group. In all instances, the rule of thumb is that these risks be articulated and understood, and that bringing what happens outside the group or feelings about it into group is a clear rule. Conflicts between subgroup members also occur outside the group. Significant and powerful issues in the recovery of group members and in the group dynamic may then be enacted outside the inner circle of safety and the unequivocal reach of the group process. Subgroup members may disclose information to each other that is hidden from what is present in the group session. Again, this may be subversive to the group process.

Some group members have felt left out by the out-of-the-group get-togethers of others. This has not always been directly expressed. In one instance where it was expressed directly, a group member said he felt left out after three others shared how much fun and how meaningful it had been for them to go to a concert together. The group member who spoke up had been feeling left out of a more subtle subgrouping within the group. However, there had been no clear situation for him to focus upon and address until this occasion. Through confronting the others about feeling left out, he was able to address and begin to handle the issue within the group.

In group one week, a nearly always congenial group member, Martin, was acting very annoyed with Alan, another member. Only after being confronted by the group did Martin acknowledge that he was hurt and angry over having been slighted by Alan's walking away from him during an after-dinner conversation before group. The conflict was thus brought into group in three steps: (1) the presentation of an affect, (2) the confrontation by the group, and (3) the acknowledgment of the conflict. The two parties then began talking, and issues that needed to be dealt with, but had not been, were opened up. Martin recognized his proneness to feel insulted, his tendency to misread cues as a result of shame-based presuppositions, and his habitual avoidance of confronting others. Alan acknowledged his proclivity not to recognize others' needs while being very sensitive about his own feelings. The misunderstanding between the two was discussed, clarified, and partially resolved. This had occurred during a phase in the group's development when aggression and anger were carefully guarded against. The aggression was taken outside of group for expression. It served as an escape valve and a springboard enabling the feelings to return to the group and be processed, deepening the sense of trust that aggressive impulses were not as dangerous or destructive as had been feared.

There is another instance in which outside-the-group contact fostered some work within the group. For months, group members had been thanking and praising one group member, Gregory, for the help and insight he gave them when they had difficulties in between group sessions. Members had often made comments to me such as "If it weren't for you and Gregory, I wouldn't be where I am today in my recovery." Though well engaged in the group process, Gregory was not self-disclosing in group and was very guarded against efforts by myself and, occasionally, by group members to give him help. In one group session, a chorus of gratitude for his help was voiced. In the context of this, and supporting his generosity and insight, I confronted him firmly with his "caretaking" and his not being receptive to help himself. This situation enabled a breakthrough of his denial. He recognized his distrust and fear of being scapegoated and shamed, as he was in his family. He recognized how he was foreclosing being receptive. He projected into the group, anticipating and reexperiencing being shamed as he was in his family, and enacted a caretaking role in response. The force of what had been taken outside the group but was being brought back in facilitated this opening-up process for Gregory.

SEXUAL ABSTINENCE

Abstinence from acting out sex- and love-addictive behaviors is not a requirement for group membership. However, drug and alcohol addictions must be in remission. Active drug and alcohol addictive behaviors preclude work on sex and love addictions, as well as work on other psychodynamic or behavioral issues. When drug and alcohol behavior is out of control, it is impossible for treatment of other issues to proceed and, for the group, the consequences are too disruptive. Occasional drug or alcohol slips—episodes of substance use that do not lead to a resumption of a cycle of drug- or alcohol-addicted patterns of thinking or behavior—by recovering drug or alcohol addicts in a sex and love addiction group are manageable and are used as part of the therapeutic process. Nonshaming confrontations, identifying triggers for a slip, support for the pain and the shame involved in the trigger and in consequence of the slip, and others sharing about slips enables the slip to be taken into the group therapeutic process. Sex and love addiction behaviors, however, are more complicated.

Some sex and love addictive behaviors of group members are clear-cut addictive behaviors. For example, John, a 35-year-old law enforcement officer, called and met with his "addictive lover." Contact with her was one of his "bottom lines," behavior that had been identified as addictive and not something he wanted to do again. When John brought this to group, he clearly recognized that this was addictive behavior. Another example is Phil, a 30-year-old bisexual, whose "bottom line" included voyeurism. Phil stood conspicuously in front of his own window and watched a neighbor undress in front of his window. He bargained with himself over whether he really violated a "bottom line." He needed clear group feedback to recognize and acknowledge that he had.

Some sex and love behaviors of recovering sex- and love-addicted group members may not be compulsive or toxic. Sexual behaviors may contain adaptive *and* maladaptive elements. Individual patterns vary considerably in the transformation from addictive to healthy sexuality. The recovery process from addicted sexuality is a gradual transition to modes of healthy sexuality. In the transition, periods of abstinence are necessary for many persons and are the surest route to recovery and healthy sexuality. However, in the transition, not acting on bottom lines and experimenting with healthy modes of sexuality may overlap in some persons.

For example, Gil, a 31-year-old airline employee, after abstinence from sexual activity for several months but still struggling with impulses toward indiscriminate, anonymous sex and other bottom lines, decided it was time for him to begin dating. This was announced in group after he had already begun dating. While there was considerable concern about his "addict" being in the driver's seat, his behavior was interpreted by the group as expressing a mixture of healthy and addictive trends, and as an attempt to steer his addictive sexual tendencies in a safer and healthier direction. In each of the ensuing relationships, Gil reported feelings of inadequacy, self-consciousness, and emotionally chasing after the other, who was presented as polite but inaccessible. The cluster of shame-related affects, out-of-control feelings, and self-destructive attachments; the inability to connect realistically; and the failure to recognize this were dysfunctional trends closely related to his history of addictive behavior patterns. However, these were occurring at a significantly higher level of ego functioning, with a far lower level of ego-disintegrative trends.

The clinical task in group involved a balancing around supporting progressive trends, helping Gil to maintain access to his reservoir of healthy self-esteem and spirituality that he and the collaborators in his recovery had nurtured, and staying attuned to the toxic shame he was trying to handle in his relationship experiences. For him, a strict rule against dating relationships would have been clinically preferable but unworkable. A strict rule might have resulted in feelings of shame and self-imposed alienation from the group. It was all too evident that his efforts to establish an intimate relationship would lead him to disappointment. The group sought to provide him safe harbor in order to prevent a cyclic fueling of addictive behavior in the face of each mounting relationship failure, and a safe space for him to begin to deal with his addiction as his recovery process evolved (and we helped it evolve) to the point where he was ready for this. It took many painful months to happen.

The exploratory edge to developing healthy sexuality in the recovering sex and love addict must be sorted out from toxic trends. For example, Mark, a 32-year-old car assembly worker, wondered if he was "love addicted" when he became intensely emotionally attached to a female peer during the first three weeks of abstinence from compulsive homosexual and heterosexual affairs. He was switching addictive acting out from sexual behaviors to relationship dependency. While relationships are healthy, this sex and love addict needed to learn how to be close to male peers before he developed an intimate relationship with a woman.

Behaviors may not be black and white. Often the difficult working through of recurring sexual actions in the therapeutic group process helps the sex and love addict to clarify bottom lines. For recovery, a nonshaming understanding of addictive sexuality and clear support of adaptive trends are needed.

One cannot psychologically assess strictly on the basis of behaviors. Assessment has to be based on the psychological function or functions of behaviors—to what extent is the sexual behavior expressing adaptive trends, and to what extent is it a recurrence of compulsive currents? When bottom lines are broken, the primary clinical responsibility is not to collude in the denial. This does not preclude our fully recognizing the intent to heal and repair shame and other injuries to the self. As recovery advances, efforts to find one's way toward a healthy relationship may be infused, confused, or influenced by regressive addictive trends. Any particular sex or love behavior of the recovering addict may be serving both progressive and regressive trends, as the above examples show. The clinical responsibility of the group therapist is to recognize both trends and provide a response to the behavior based on an assessment of what will foster recovery and growth.

SHAME OF THE FATHER

The most significant, pervasive, determinative feature in the group-as-a-whole is shame. Shame that was originally (developmentally) experienced by members in their relation to their fathers appears to be at the heart of the group dynamic. The legacy of the father's shame in the shame of the son appears in group as the apparent precipitant of the development of addictive behaviors in members. In the group itself, this shame legacy seems to be the core of the forces that shape the group process. Diverse features of the group process evidence the underlying shame dynamic. Steven, a 32-year-old schoolteacher whose father's legacy to him was a sense of helplessness, shame, and suspicion that women were out to manipulate and control him, developed a shame-based hyperreceptivity to any wish he perceived or projected in interactions with women. He felt demands that threatened to take his manly value from him and to overwhelm him. A primary feature of his addiction was that whenever he experienced sexual interest from a woman, he would feel frightened and overwhelmed by her control and power. In order to extricate himself, he experienced uncontrolled spontaneous ejaculation. This served the purpose of releasing him from bondage to her sexuality. The shame Steven felt as a consequence was the return of the shame that precipitated ejaculation. The anxiety experienced by this sex and love addict is a variation on an anxiety at the core of the interactive matrix of the group. The group is the sanctuary from shame-based dangers of human interaction for members, while at the same time the undercurrent threat in the group dynamic is experienced as a representation of these dangers.

In one group session, Tim gave another member feedback on how to handle a situation. Another group member, Chris, gave opposite advice. Tim became angry. He confronted Chris, saying there was no reason that Chris had to say he was wrong. Chris became enraged and told Tim not to tell him what he could and couldn't say. Another group member, Mario, became frightened and confused, felt a loss of boundaries, and sensed something inside him was out of control. The group member who had received the advice felt guilty, and the others in group were choosing sides. The entire group, each in his own role, was reacting to the presence of "father shame" in the group. When I pointed this out, the group immediately recognized that each party to the conflict was experiencing the other as his shaming father. Tim and Chris had each experienced the other's comments as invalidating them, just as their fathers had done. That issue, like the conflict and high tension that erupted in the group, emerged in the group process from an always latently present and evolving group anxiety. In this anxiety, group members experience themselves as controlled, enraged, humiliated, exposed, worthless, abandoned, helpless, violated, and shamed by a denying and projecting father.

SHAME AND NARCISSISTIC VULNERABILITY

Ambivalence in the group interpersonal relationships and in the conflicting valences of wishing to draw close and to distance are indicative more of the shame-based organization of the group dynamic than of underlying guilt. Shame-based ambivalence charges the group with a particularly intense narcissistic vulnerability. Members' wish to relate and be known is countered by exposure anxiety. Concealed narcissistic rage sets up a fragile boundary vulnerability felt between members, with a consequent tendency for members to "make nice" and feel anxious about hurting the feelings of others. The underlying shame anxiety here, based on the core group belief of being flawed and defective human beings, saturates the group experience. The situation described above, in which two group members reacted to each other with the hurt and fury that originated in their experience of their father's shame, is a good example of this core group vulnerability and belief. Core vulnerability and shame rage are present in the proneness of sex and love addicts, each due to his own shame, to misinterpret each other.

A narcissistically secure environment needs to be nurtured gradually in group. Care needs to be exercised by attending to narcissistic injuries when they occur. Developing group norms that are empathetic is a primary concern in establishing a therapeutic environment. Paul, a group member whose sex and love addiction had a masochistic theme, early in his history with the group showed a penchant for making others angry, for being annoying, and for defusing group tension by drawing ire upon himself. Paul was the inevitable target for aggressive and shaming projections that the group had difficulty containing. He was characterologically well suited to meet the group scapegoating needs. He was criticized for his unwashed clothes in one session, for his inappropriate humor in many sessions, for interrupting others, for intellectualizing and lecturing, and for his diverse techniques for provoking anger. In developing safe and nurturing group norms, it was critical that Paul and the group not be permitted to succeed in the ritual enactment of shaming him and fixing him in the outcast role.

Not only for his sake but also as a therapeutic task in his treatment in group, it was important to put an end to his long history of being defiled and cast out; it was also significant because he represented the outcast in each and every group member. If Paul was not safe, no sex and love addict was safe in the group.

An empathic group norm to protect against core injuries to the sense of self was fostered in several ways. The scapegoating by the group was pointed out and the anxieties projected onto the scapegoat identified. The addictive "acting in" behavior of the scapegoat was likewise pointed out, and the pain, conflicts, shame, and acting-out patterns associated with it were discussed in group. Those who were drawn into Paul's web of masochistic self-sacrifice were helped to recognize their own issues. His injured feelings were attended to with concern. While he played the fool, he was treated with dignity.

The overriding need for affirmation among members is a significant nurturing process in the development of the group. One evening, David, a 28-year-old sex and love addict, began his group time by sharing a list of affirmations that he had developed while in residential treatment. He said, "I deserve my recovery. I am a worthy human being, and I care about myself. I deserve to be happy. I deserve to be treated with respect."

Validation and support come to be truly experienced in confrontation as well as in affirmation only when there is a well-developed level of trust in the group. Shame boundaries need to have been secured so the group-as-a-whole is no longer functioning in a primarily shame-prone mode. This transformation from shame-based group dynamics to healthy self-esteem is a basic therapeutic process in this group.

Shame-related affects and cognitions are defended against by compulsive thinking and compulsive behaviors (acting out), denial, and dissociation. In the group dynamics, as described by Bion (1974), behaviors such as "fight-flight" or "pairing" function as defenses against the core shame anxieties in group. The vulnerability to being shamed in group is nearly as virulent as the sexual addiction itself. Actually, the therapeutic capacity of the group to contain the shame vulnerability of its members is its capacity to contain (i.e., provide a safe and therapeutic space for resolving) the sex and love addictions of group members. The functional identity of sex and love addiction and shame vulnerability in group reflects the shame-based origin of sex and love addiction. The group tends to function therapeutically in treating sex and love addiction of members when group empathic acceptance transforms shame and narcissistic vulnerability by affirming that one is really valued.

SHAME AND THE GROUP THERAPIST

The vulnerability of group members to being shamed, to hiding, to displacing and raging over fragments of experience that have been infused with a shame disturbance presents a particular set of clinical demands upon the group therapist. The clinical management of this sensitive terrain by the construction and maintenance of secure shame boundaries requires that the therapist's own underlying shame legacy and propensities be accessible to him or her.

Sex and love addict group therapists need to be or become sufficiently free of shame toxicity and inhibition that may be present in their own sexuality, their relationships with members of the same sex, and their self-relation. Unresolved shame about a therapist's father or his or her shame in the father's eyes will complicate and compromise his or her therapeutic openness to, and ability to provide a therapeutic container for, the sometimes subtle and varied manifestations of shame within the group. The issues of the therapist need careful, prudent, and honest attention. The honesty of group members is the key to their recovery. The honesty of the therapist is the cornerstone of his or her discipline.

Powerful psychotherapeutic forces are brought alive in the group, in each group member, and the group therapist. The therapist needs to cultivate a place within, between expression and inhibition, in order to be aware. Growth in differentiated awareness of the therapeutic field is the inevitable outcome of continued processing of therapeutic experience in groups. The clinical neutrality, as defined by Kernberg (1965), of the therapist does not mean an absence of experiencing his or her own emotional reality vis-à-vis the undertow and overt pull of the group dynamic. It means being there, present with the process with no less honesty than is prescribed for group members. It means processing a multidimensional field of individual and group dynamics that includes the pivotal functions of his or her own perceptual processes.

Awareness of my own shame-based interferences with my therapeutic role is provided by developing signals in my internal feedback loop that I am exerting energy to inhibit experiencing an affect or cognition. Inhibition of experience results in (a) failure to have perceptual information about the emotional meaning of some event in group; (b) communications that will inhibit, complicate, or violate group members; (c) failure to process the existence and meaning of his event for one's internal record of the group and the course of events in group; and (d) not being able to manage the inhibited parts of the experience for group members and the group-as-a-whole.

The most frequent signal to myself that I am subjectively inhibiting something in the group dynamic is my feeling that I need to control something in the group. The second most common signal is being distracted. The third most common signal is a sense of internal pressure or stress. The fourth most common signal/experience is the sense of being out of sync with the group. I have done a lot of work on the shame-based features of my relationship with my father, my self-worth, and my sexuality. I believe that this work has helped to fine-tune my awareness of and sensitivity to these issues in group.

The primitive and subversive affects of sex and love addiction can be invisible and insidious in group. For example, a group member named Rick recounted a sexual incident that was compulsive and functioned to pervasively deny the pain of his father's emotional abuse. I felt a need to confront his denial. I thought that Rick's facing his denial would foster his ability to manage the pain he was in and to grow through it, but my interventions were ignored by the group.

In the face of my failure to connect with him or any other group member, I was compelled to check out my assumptions. I recognized that I was threatened by the feelings of overwhelming helplessness and being out of control that he was frantically denying. In acting to help Rick confront his denial, I was using him to control my own helplessness and anxiety: I was denying the shame of helplessness that was communicated to and resonated in me. Further, it became clear that his helplessness was experienced as the other person's desiring him and controlling him through desire. His account of this resonated through the group with meaningfulness in diverse ways. I felt his agony and the wish to stop his pain. Instead of using this as a signal for self-reflection, I was prompted to act by helplessness and shame over the helplessness his account triggered in me.

Being aware of shame potentials in group requires operating out of a sufficiently developed, healthy shame in oneself. The therapist's ability to avoid shaming members, denying the existence or priority of protective shame needs, colluding in hiding shame, and failing to recognize the shame-based origin of group disturbance requires careful attention, gentleness, and openness to oneself. The development of the therapist over the course of conducting a sex and love addicts' therapy group is most likely to be in his or her capacity to help the group to deepen and expand their healthy and protective shame.

Healthy shame is the secure shame boundary that protects against exposure and self-consciousness. It may be evidenced in acting with discretion, humility, or modesty, and in self-confidence. In the healing process, the group can implicitly heal the therapist and strengthen his or her protective shame capacity. It may be a source of gratitude that the therapist feels toward the group. It may otherwise constitute implicit mutuality and respect in the therapeutic relationship of the therapist and the group.

The shame of the father as the core of the group dynamic protectively invests the therapeutic risks and possibilities of the group's shame in the group therapist. Maintaining a group space in which the men's internalized shame in the eyes of their fathers (shamed by their fathers' toxic shame) can be safely experienced and transformed requires that the therapist's healthy shame safely contain the toxic shame anxieties of the group. The devaluations, humiliations, identity diffusions, and disintegrative anxieties associated with the violation of shame boundaries by their fathers propels a cycle of shame in the self's experience of itself and its relation to others. This shame cycle is regenerated in the recurring cycle of addictive sexuality. Group space that is a hospitable shelter to the diverse, persistent, captious, and troublesome pain of the shame-based sexual turmoil of group members requires a nonjudgmental empathic valuing of the humanity, dignity, and grace of group members.

CLOSENESS/DISTANCE AMONG GROUP MEMBERS

There is among the men in a sex and love addiction group a need to relate to and be close to other men. The realization of this need is an important step in their treatment. This need is multiply determined. In part, it reflects a far-reaching and general societal need for men to develop relationships with other men. This need is especially present for the sex and love addicted men who have been severely wounded by their fathers.

Sex- and love-addicted men have tended to avoid emotional intimacy in all relations with other people. In relating to others, they function out of compulsivity and otherwise tend to be cut off and alienated from persons with whom they interact. Sex- and love-addicted persons do not, strictly speaking, have a "relationship" with their sexual partners. A relationship implies the recognition of a separate person to whom one relates. The sex- and love-addicted person's sexual partner is the object of an addictive urge. For example, a sex and love addict had sex with another man in a pornographic bookstore. He said the encounter made him feel loved and accepted. He fantasized about their relationship and their becoming a couple. In another instance, a sex and love addict was constantly frustrated by his girlfriend's demands and by not getting his needs met. She either satisfied his needs or frustrated them, but she did not exist separate from his needs.

Sex and love addiction is a relationship avoidance stratagem of the human spirit rooted in and fueled by a profound alienation from and distrust of others. Several of the men in one group, whose sex and love addiction involved compulsive sexuality, at some point in their recovery became unable to detach from relationships that were increasingly emotionally abusive, that is, they became love addicted. As caretakers and approval seekers, these men were not yet relating to a separate person but were using the other to get their needs met and avoiding the mutuality of a love relationship. Fear of the repetition of the unhealed wounds inflicted by the father makes relationships threatening. The need for closeness and the fear of closeness with other men form a potent undercurrent in the group dynamic.

Group interaction behavior in the ongoing negotiating of closeness/ distance resembles the rapprochement subphase on Mahler's (1979) separation-individuation developmental line. It should be noted that the shame-based relationship with the father, which tends to be focal and pivotal among the men in the sex and love addicts group, is built upon an early bonding experience with the mother that tends to be fraught with boundary violation, overindulgence, or emotional abandonment, and mistrust that serves as a foundation for the shame-faulty identification with the father.

Harold, a 40-year-old black professional, spoke at length one evening about his feelings of never fitting in anywhere. He did not fit into the white world and was also uncomfortable with the "rap and jive of black parties." In terms of gender identity, as a bisexual, Harold did not fit clearly into the gay world or the straight life. Others in the group were able to identify with the feeling of not fitting in. Sex and love addicts commonly feel that they do not fit in. This is, however, basically due more to developmental issues than to their life-style: "I always have felt that I didn't really fit in, that I was different, even when I was a kid. I learned to develop an outward way of acting, so people don't see it, but my true self feels like an alien."

The need for closeness in group and the fear of exposure and abandonment strike a familiar chord for sex and love addicts, and play a significant role in the vicissitudes of the group process. Needing to bond, needing to find acceptance and mutuality, and fearing exclusion and abandonment, members feel a need to draw close. Drawing close, they feel threatened and overwhelmed, and are infused with abandonment anxiety, loss-of-self anxiety, and primitive aggression/annihilation anxiety. A heightened sense of shame vulnerability is aroused. Group members react to incipient closeness by pulling back from each other, reducing interactive contact and trust, and putting up barriers.

Within the context of this recurring pattern, as members come to experience increased levels of trust and safety within group, and as the closeness/distance conflict is reduced, normative friendship intimacy develops. At the close of the session in which he shared his feelings of not belonging, Harold stated that he felt "relieved" and "closer to the group." By having talked about it and having the feeling accepted and mirrored in group, his feeling of not fitting in was taken into the group process. While his "relief" was only momentary, it fostered his therapeutic bonding with the group and engaged a process of beginning to resolve the developmental failures he has experienced.

With this population social isolation is not due solely to the secrecy characteristic of sex and love addiction. The addict's tendency for isolation presents in group in a multilayered way. As group members become more open and connected, deeper layers of isolation, aloneness, and abandonment may gradually become evident. One evening, Joe, a group member, reported that with his growing sense of confidence and being able to relate to other people as friends, he is beginning to realize just how insecure and isolated he had felt. He said that now he can see how cut off he still is. He reported that he felt more connected to everyone in the group but can now recognize how unimportant and ignored he feels in group. "It had been so much a part of me, I was never aware of it before." The "unfelt feeling" of not connecting with others had inhibited his experience of other people.

Along with a deeper aloneness being realized, the need for being vulnerable in group may also evolve. In the progressive sense of closeness and friendship among group members, pseudo intimacy may function defensively against closeness or aggression. In one newly formed group, the undercurrent of anxiety was strong. The underlying anxiety was, as is normal in the early phase of group development, about relationship boundaries in the group and about aggression. In the midst of this, members were behaving and talking to each other with a heightened sense of closeness. This pseudo intimacy functioned to ward off feelings of overwhelming anxiety. The closeness/distance patterns among members may resemble breathing as members internalize and externalize. When the group is anxious, rapid internalizing/externalizing may occur.

DISSOCIATIVE TRENDS

In the love- and sex-addicted person, clusters of self associated with the addiction—cognitions, affects, and behaviors—may present as dissociated from nonaddictive personality traits. In the development of the addiction, a partially dissociated identity develops. Sex and love addicts refer to the actions, thoughts, and feelings that are part of addictive behavior patterns as if the agent were a separate, autonomous identity. This dissociated identity is sometimes referred to as "the addict" or the feeling of "being in my addict." For example, "I was driving to the bank when I saw a very attractive woman, just my type. She looked at me. I was gone. You know, before I knew it, I was in my addict." Being in one's addict may also be employed as a therapeutic stratagem. Carnes (1989) describes it as a tool the client may use to talk about his or her addiction in order to gain therapeutic leverage.

In the group-as-a-whole, collective dissociated processes may be evidenced progressively or regressively. Progressively, group dynamics and developments are geared primarily toward integration of parts of the self that are caught in the compulsive tyranny of addictive functioning. Regressively, the group can conspire in the service of the wily tyrant (the addict), aimed at maintaining the addict's power by denying it (not admitting it to consciousness). In the regressive mode, addictive thoughts and affects are unsanctioned and invisible in group space. Affirmations are really not affirmations but denials. For example, after Tim reported an incident in which he was "in his addict" and committed an unequivocal violation of a primary bottom line, another group member affirmed his risk-taking and courage. The group-as-a-whole was in a denial phase. The rest of the group buoyed and reiterated Tim's denial and the member who first supported him. No group member acknowledged that Tim had been out of control and needed to abstain from bottom-line behaviors. The group dressed up their unified denial as an affirmation. The attempt by the group therapist to call this into question was dismissed as a bothersome and ignorant thing that therapists do.

Group space constituted by dissociative dynamics is a shame-based splitting off of the out-of-control addicted self. In this group space, the shameful compulsivity of the addict is everywhere—and nowhere. Excluded from group by shame, its threat is pervasive in group interactions. It is excluded but persists as the primitive affective core of the group dynamic. It returns to group experience as recurring anxiety or affective disturbance in the life of the group. One form of this is the way in which feelings of humiliation and narcissistic rage are always ready to surface and the constant, if not always evident, pressure on the surface of the group process that comes from these underlying feelings. The group excludes such feelings as too threatening to the security and bond of the group but readmits them periodically.

The therapeutic viability of the group will depend upon a regulation of these anxieties that prevents them from endangering the group cohesion while allowing their release into the group. Processing these feelings in this way is a key therapeutic dimension of the group. Fragments of the "affective core" shame are expressed and reintegrated into the developing therapeutic potency of the group. Vulnerability to this underlying shame, at other times in the life history of the group, may inhibit members from being in touch with themselves or from self-disclosure. In a more radical way for some group members and for some groups, the threat of annihilation by shame may create a sense of no-self or a disturbing and elusive vacuum in the group. Shame-based secretiveness, hiding and concealing from others and from oneself, employs and strengthens dissociative functions of the self. The same is true of the group process.

The therapeutic process in group involves the reversal of this trend and the progressive reintegration of the shame-ridden sexual aspects of the self. A desperate shame-sexuality is an integral part of the addicted self. Addictive sexuality is rooted developmentally in a shame-injured aspect of one's identity. Phenomenologically, sex- and love-addictive behavior patterns express a shame-based sense of powerlessness, worthlessness, or abandonment anxiety; a discharge of shame-rage or associated primitive anxieties; a dysregulative stimulus-boundary; or related feelings of being overwhelmed or out of control. The addictive act has the aim of stopping the pain. The compulsive repeating of the pain in the very act that aims to end it fosters dissociative thinking.

Early in his recovery, Calvin, a 24-year-old store clerk, sat home on a Saturday night, sinking deeper and deeper into loneliness and self-loathing. His recovery beliefs, affirmations, and feelings of self-worth were out of reach. He felt he was his old self. As these feelings grew stronger, Calvin came to be "in his addict." He called an outcall prostitution service. The addictive action sought to ease his pain; at the same time, it reinforced his sense of emptiness and worthlessness. Dissociative thought processes were exercised by maintaining the belief that the addictive behavior was making him better while its internal reality and significance were self-destructive. This is how the cognitive base for the addictive cycle is cultivated. Group treatment provides a safe, nurturing space for the sex and love addict to develop a feedback loop that breaks down the dissociative cognition.

MIRRORING

Another powerful therapeutic function of group psychotherapy for sex- and love-addicted persons is its capacity to foster the progressive reintegration of dissociated sexual aspects of oneself. The British group psychotherapist Foulkes (1965) has noted and conceptualized the mirroring function of groups. The mirror in group psychotherapy for sex- and love-addicted men is the group dynamic of mutual recognition. In this mirror, group members come to experience themselves not only in the eyes of the other members and the group-as-a-whole, but also through recognizing themselves in the others, including the shame-dissociated, addicted aspects of themselves.

Group members frequently are aware of and comment upon recognizing some part of themselves in another group member. This also occurs at a deeper level of the self. One group member spoke about his father's subtle way of devaluing all his accomplishments and his father's need to control him. Around the circle, group members identified with feelings of being devalued by their fathers, some linking this explicitly to their addiction: "My acting out with multiple affairs was really my trying to prove my worth to my father. He made me feel I couldn't do anything right. He never, ever recognized anything I did. I couldn't let anyone know who I was, because they'd see I was really nothing. Nothing! I had to keep running from that."

The identity diffusion and flight from self of the sex and love addict is reflected and contained around the circle through the identification experienced by members. Individual identity is nurtured through positive group identification based in a common realization of loss of self (shame-based identity). Group members can find themselves in the group mirror.

The mirroring function may enable group members to experience themselves, helping on the pathway toward self-acceptance and reintegration of alienated parts of oneself. In being a member of a group, one's likeness to others in the group is implicit, and may gradually evolve toward a mutual empathic recognition and acceptance of the self. Self-recognition and self-acceptance are a normative outcome of group mirroring as a group develops toward a higher level of empathy and mutuality. Paul, a member who had a proclivity for being the group scapegoat, was mentioned earlier in this chapter. As Paul began to find love and acceptance in the group, he gradually started to develop greater self-acceptance. In the transformation of his behavior from controlling others in a masochistic reenactment of a profoundly shameful abandonment that had become the core of his sense of self, he began to joke about himself in benign, forgiving ways that reflected his newly developing self-acceptance. Catching himself as he began to taunt the group into rejecting him, he said, "I'm talking so much just to bother you all." Then he laughed. Others laughed with him. He was able to listen attentively to others and to engage in empathic, interactive, and connected exchanges with other group members.

CONCLUSION

In this chapter some basic group process themes for groups of male sex and love addicts have been addressed. Clinical implications of group membership and belongingness that underlie the therapeutic effectiveness of the group are considered. Membership secures the difficult recovery process and fosters the integrative norms of the group as the nucleus of the recovering self. Several themes in the setup of the group are focused on: rituals, outside-the-group contact, and sexual abstinence. These are topics that concern the clinical management of the recovery process through group structures and a disciplined flexibility in containing addictive trends and fostering adaptive, healthy recovery initiatives.

The central clinical issue of recovery is shame. Three dimensions of shame in the group were reviewed: (1) the core developmental shame legacy of the father, (2) the narcissistic vulnerability and identity diffusion of the self of group members, and (3) the significance of the group therapist's shame. Understanding the delicate, pervasive, and pivotal shame-based group dynamic issues is the key to securing and maintaining the therapeutic efficacy of the group process.

Finally, a cluster of group process themes was presented: (1) the closeness/distance dynamic, (2) dissociative thought processes, and (3) mirroring. Relationship to self and to others in the group, subjective and intersubjective dimensions of the process, are recognized as the matrix of recovery.

The integration of a solid theoretical group therapy framework, a general understanding of the addictive process, and the specific issues of sex and addiction guide our approach to group psychotherapy with sex- and love-addicted men.

Finally, I wish to state my gratitude to the sex- and love-addicted men whose pain and courage have taught me about sexual addictions, therapeutic group process with sexual addictions, and our common humanity. I have grown, and my ideas have been shaped into the ideas presented here, through the tenacity of both the addictive and the recovery process that has informed the group experience. The struggle of these men toward recovery continues to challenge my perspective and understanding.

REFERENCES

Agazarian, Yvonne, ed. (1989). "Special Issue: The Group-as-a-Whole." *Group* 13, no. 3–4.
Ashbach, Charles, and Schermer, Victor. (1987). *Object Relations, the Self and the Group: A Conceptual Paradigm.* London: Routledge and Kegan Paul.
Bion, Wilfred R. (1974). *Experience in Groups.* New York: Ballantine Books.

Carnes, Patrick. (1989). *Contrary to Love*. Minneapolis: CompCare.

Foulkes, S. H. (1965). *Therapeutic Group Analysis*. New York: International Universities Press.

Griffin-Shelley, Eric. (1991). *Sex and Love: Addiction Treatment and Recovery*. New York: Praeger.

Kernberg, Otto. (1965). *Borderline Personality Disorders and Pathological Narcissism*. New York: Jason Aronson.

Langs, Robert. (1976). *The Therapeutic Interaction*, vols. 1 and 2. New York: Jason Aronson.

Mahler, Margaret. (1979). *On Human Symptoms and the Vicissitudes of Individuation*, I, *Infantile Psychosis*. New York: International Universities Press.

CHAPTER 6

Women's Issues in Addiction Recovery

Linda Dubrow

My observations on women's issues in recovery from sex and love addiction are based on my work with female clients in individual therapy in my private practice, and in group therapy, which was part of the intensive, outpatient therapy program described in Chapter 2.

I led two groups in the intensive, outpatient therapy program. A long-term therapy group was offered for women without making a distinction between who was sexually addicted and who was love or relationship dependent. A short-term group was offered for women emotionally involved with sex/love-addicted people. I will refer to the long-term therapy group for sex and love addicts as "the group," and will specify when I am referring to the short-term group for co-addicts.

Mental health professionals have tried to distinguish between sex addiction and love or relationship dependency. This has typically resulted in men being diagnosed as sex addicted and women as love or relationship dependent. This dichotomy is well entrenched in cultural norms, in which women are often defined according to their relationships with men, and men are seen as preoccupied with sexual conquest. Carnes (1991) reported that women felt they had learned as children that "A woman simply is no good without a boyfriend" (p. 157), and referred to the cultural expectation that "boys will be boys" (p. 29). At times, when some men express interest in committed relationships, or some women express sexual interests outside the context of committed relationships, people greet these non-stereotyped responses with ridicule or derision.

In the intensive outpatient program, we treated sex and love addiction as one diagnosis. We believed that the men and women had similar treatment needs, and provided analogous treatment for both sexes. Only the therapy groups were segregated by sex.

The women felt strongly about their preference for a women's therapy group, and preferred a female leader. In a few instances in which I was unable to lead the group, the members did not want to be combined with a men's group or to be led by the male supervising therapist. At times, the women felt stimulated by the presence of men to whom they felt attracted during the psychoeducational group that preceded the therapy group. Similar problems were experienced in the sexually integrated Twelve Step meetings. Some women reported being asked out by men, or even kissed goodnight following a meeting. While I believed that it was helpful for men and women to attend psychoeducational and Twelve Step groups together so that they could have the potential for nonsexual, nonromantic relationships with the opposite sex, I also encouraged the women to attend at least one Twelve Step meeting that was women only. The women followed this suggestion, and tended to feel most safe and comfortable in the women's meetings.

DEFINING THE POPULATION

The diagnosis of sex addiction is more frequently assigned to men than to women. At times, there is a different flavor to the expression of sex and/or love addictions in men and women. For example, men tend to be arrested more frequently for sexually-acting-out behaviors than women. Women presenting with sex- and love-addicted-related behaviors tend to be diagnosed as having related mental health difficulties, such as depression or bipolar disorder, rather than as having their addiction.

The women in the therapy group were screened for their appropriateness in the group by the program's founder, Eric Griffin-Shelley. They presented a variety of behaviors and circumstances. Some of the women were dually diagnosed, having addictions and other mental health disorders, the most frequent being bipolar disorder. The dually diagnosed women received treatment for their other mental health problems through individual psychotherapy, family therapy, and/or psychotropic medication; the intensive, outpatient group therapy program focused on their addiction issues.

Characteristics of the female clients included moving from one relationship to another quickly and with a frenetic desperation; quick and intense involvement in a new relationship; remaining in a relationship that was destructive even after becoming aware of this destructiveness; taking unusual risks in order to become or remain involved with the person; and otherwise behaving like an addict in what might be called the "lying, cheating, and stealing syndrome": "Sex and love addicts steal time, attention, affection, and money from their families, and share their ill-gotten gains with their addictive acquaintances" (Griffin-Shelley, 1991, p. 63).

Many of the women had engaged in criminal behavior at the initiative and prodding of their partners, although these same women were usually law-abiding and had not engaged in illegal activity outside their addictive relationships. For example, one woman allowed her partner to set a fire in her house, so that they could split an insurance payment. Another woman set up robbery victims for her boyfriend by flirting with them, thereby distracting them. Stealing in sex and love addiction may include the concept of "stealing" an unavailable (married or committed) sex partner.

The difficulties in distinguishing between sex addiction and love addiction were demonstrated by the complexities of the behaviors of our clients. Sex addiction in women sometimes masqueraded as a love addiction because the women appeared to be involved in a monogamous relationship. For example, when I referred a woman for inpatient treatment, she was placed in a women's intervention unit rather than the sex addiction unit because her presenting problem was that she was unable to disengage herself from one particular man, despite many deleterious effects of the relationship upon her life. Her ability to function at work and as a mother had been diminished to the point where she was at some risk of losing her job or being charged with child neglect. She had been involved with the man for several months, but she obsessed about him constantly, and had unprotected sex with him. To outsiders, the negative points of this relationship were obvious: he was much younger, was unemployed, and appeared to be addicted to drugs. The client became aware of these points but was unable to say "no" even to outrageous requests (demands) from him, including participation in illegal behavior and providing money that he spent on other women. She allowed the man's brother to stay with them, the implications of which will be discussed later, and sometimes she gave money or shelter to his friends or drug dealers. She remained in the relationship even after he became physically abusive to her, and after he was emotionally abusive to her daughter. Despite all this, she appeared to be involved in a monogamous relationship and therefore was not seen in the same light, or as having the same disease, as men who compulsively act out sexually.

The problems resulting from her placement in a women's unit rather than in the sex addiction unit became most evident at the time of discharge.

She was not required to sign a contract to attend 90 Sex and Love Addicts Anonymous (SLAA) meetings in 90 days, or to commit to a period of abstinence from sexual/romantic relationships, as would have been asked of her upon discharge from the sexual addiction unit. Her plan to be picked up at the airport by a former boyfriend was not criticized, although it was like a heroin addict being picked up at a drug rehabilitation program and getting a fix in the car. Within two weeks, she had been sexual with the person who picked her up at the airport, and the man she had been obsessing about when she was hospitalized. She had unprotected sex with both.

Her sex addiction continued to become more apparent as she decompensated. Unfortunately, another problem during her hospitalization was an inappropriate change in her medication. She had been taking lithium for years. However, this was challenged by the hospital psychiatrist, who discontinued her lithium and prescribed an antidepressant. Within a month of her discharge, she experienced a manic episode and became psychotic. She was involuntarily hospitalized. The first night at the hospital, she angrily tried to jam some papers into her vagina during a physical examination. She eventually had to be placed in restraints. Another night, she had to sleep on a bench because there were no beds available; she did not stop another patient, also sleeping on a bench, from reaching over and fondling her genitals. Thus, when she decompensated and came under extreme stress, she acted more like the stereotypical male sex addict.

The diagnosis of sex/love addiction could have been easily missed for another client who came to group without being in an active relationship. She had recently ended a relationship with a man that appeared to have been unhealthy and self-destructive. She was able to abstain from seeing men for months. However, all the time that she was not seeing anyone, she was planning a vacation during which she expected to allow herself, as she usually did, the freedom to have sex whenever she wanted with whomever she wanted, like the alcoholic who celebrates his/her sobriety with a drink. Although she promised her individual therapist that on her next vacation she would at least stick to the bottom line of abstaining from unprotected sex, she failed to do so. Since her partner was a stranger, and they were alone in his house, she was afraid that he might respond violently to a refusal to his request for unprotected sex. Powerless to say no, she risked both pregnancy and diseases.

The diagnosis of this woman was complicated by the variations in her outward behavior at different times during a cyclical pattern of sexual addiction and sexual anorexia (compulsive abstinence). Because of her "dry spells," she looked like a binge or episodic sexaholic. However, the level of obsession during her periods of abstinence cast suspicion on the label of episodic addiction. Despite the cyclical nature of her sexual acting-out behaviors, she was constantly preoccupied with sexual encounters in her mental life.

Another client had been involved with one man for over ten years. One night she became angry at him because he chose to be with his other girlfriend rather than with her. By sheer chance, a man dialed her telephone number by mistake, and engaged her in a conversation that led to an invitation to meet on a street corner. Although she stated, "I'm not that kind of woman," she nevertheless was seduced into agreeing to meet him.

The behavior of the first client during her casual sexual encounter with a stranger at the hospital, of the second client during her vacations, and of the third client when she was getting ready to meet the stranger differ in a striking manner compared with their behaviors at other times. There may be a positive correlation between an increase in the level of relationship stress experienced by the women and their behaviors becoming more sexual and less relationship oriented.

For purposes of treatment, it did not appear necessary or even particularly helpful to make distinctions between sex and love addiction. Although the addicts were seen separately from co-addicts, many of the underlying issues were the same, including (a) a preoccupation with sex, whether it was their own sexual activity or the activity of the partner; (b) separation/individuation issues; (c) fear of abandonment; and (d) a dysfunctional family background. The similarity in issues was so striking that it is even possible that a combined therapy group for female sex and love addicts and co-addicts might be effective.

RESISTANCE TO TREATMENT

It was difficult to get women referred to the group, to get women to join the group, and to get women to remain in the group. There was resistance not only by the women themselves but also by therapists, doctors, and family members, to identify the problem as sex and/or love addiction. As is evident in the above examples, it is easy to misdiagnose these problems in women. Therapists and others can spend considerable time dealing with other issues, such as bipolar disorder or depression, which seemed to be common alternative diagnoses given by other mental health professionals, or relationship issues, without labeling these issues as addictive in nature or as seeing the clients as needing to be dually diagnosed. Without adding the perspective of addiction, clients can improve on their other issues, but they tend not to be relieved of their obsession or able to change their addiction-related behaviors.

When friends, family members, and mental health professionals did not view the problem as an addictive one, it was easy for them to advocate looking for the "right" man or a better relationship to help the person to get over a recent loss. This message is further magnified in the popular media, which often positively portray a quick "recovery" from a failed relationship by replacing the lost partner. The addiction perspective suggested advocating a period of abstinence from romantic/sexual relationships, which fostered the opportunity for the person to mourn the loss of earlier relationships, feel okay on her own without a partner, foster self-esteem, and reexperience the personal pain that was masked, pushed down, and denied by the acting-out behaviors.

Twelve Step meetings and the peer support offered in them seemed to provide a necessary adjunct to therapy. Our groups were unlike traditional psychotherapy groups in that members' contact outside the group sessions was encouraged. These contacts were often very effective in enhancing self-esteem, diminishing feelings of loneliness and shame, decreasing the isolation that frequently fuels addictive behavior, and helping clients to control their impulsive urges.

We must keep in mind that in our culture, it is difficult for a woman to admit to wanting or needing sex in the ways that have been expected of men, let alone admit that they are powerless over these feelings. Sex purely for the sake of enjoyment, as opposed to relationship or procreation, is often still negatively judged for women. Historically, women have been less resistant than men to seeking outpatient treatment for a variety of problems, including depression, anxieties, or phobias (Chesler, 1972; McGrath et al., 1990). However, they tend to be more resistant than men to seeking help in inpatient addiction rehabilitation centers and outpatient addiction-related counseling, with the exception of compulsive overeating or other eating disorders, and co-addiction or codependency (Carnes, 1991).

MULTIPLE ADDICTIONS

Frequently, addictions do not occur in isolation; rather, the individual exhibits a number of addictions, either concurrently or successively. Usually one of the addictions can be labeled as the primary addiction, at least at any particular time, and this needs to be treated first. In Carnes's (1991) predominantly male (82 percent) sample of sex addicts, 42 percent had a chemical dependency, 38 percent had an eating disorder, 28 percent worked compulsively, and 26 percent were compulsive spenders. For female sex and love addicts, in the samples I have treated, the most frequent multiple addiction tended to be to food, or compulsive overeating. Childhood sexual abuse has been documented as an etiological factor in the development of both eating disorders (Bass & Davis, 1988) and sexual acting-out behaviors (Carnes, 1991).

I have experience in working with both food addiction and sex and love addiction. I have found that food addicts often have associated problems with body and sexual image. I have observed that all the food addicts with whom I have worked had sex- and love-addiction-related issues, although not necessarily to the level of a true addiction, while not all of the sex and love addicts had food addiction issues. One woman who was struggling with both food and sex and love addiction commented, "I seem to have trouble with any natural body functions."

The women in the therapy group I led tended to attend Twelve Step meetings both for love and sex addiction (SLAA) and for compulsive overeating (Overeaters Anonymous). While they frequently found that both sets of behaviors were out of control concurrently, it was also not unusual for only food or only sex and love to be out of control at a particular time. A period of abstinence from sex and love addiction tended to lead to an increase in compulsive overeating, and vice versa. One woman stated that she had no reason to keep her weight down when she was abstaining from relationships with men. When the women achieved abstinence from food addiction, they tended to lose weight, which led to their feeling more sexually attractive. Some women bought new clothing during these times, and became more preoccupied with looking attractive. The weight loss actually did seem to lead to an increase in attention from men, and the women tended to be more aware of this attention, all of which supported romantic intrigue and tended to lead to sexual acting-out behaviors. Virtue (1989) has described a "yo-yo syndrome" in which people's weight goes up and down; the alternation between food and sex/love addiction could be considered a "yo-yo syndrome" in its own right, in which two normal drives go awry.

An additional complicating factor was that some women who are addicted to sex/love and/or food also are, or become, addicted to shopping. Some of the female sex- and love-addicted clients also attended Twelve Step meetings of Debtors Anonymous. The need for new clothes resulting from weight loss sometimes leads to a shopping spree and out-of-control spending. The media are full of sexually seductive advertising that seems to promise sex, love, acceptance, and self-esteem if certain products are bought. Wesson (1990) described "retail seduction," in which stores try to attract people to go there and to stay there longer, increasing the probability of sales. Depressed women seemed to be targeted in certain ads that promised increased vitality and energy. The compulsion to shoplift, or kleptomania, might be viewed as a variation of the shopping addiction, and was mentioned with some regularity by female sex and love addicts. Some women stole from candy stores, even though they had money to pay, or took food from other people's refrigerators. A more subtle example of stealing was when a woman compulsively ate an entire cake that she had prepared for a relative's birthday party.

Many multiple addicts reported that recovery from food, sex and love, and/or shopping addiction(s) was more difficult than recovery from other addictions because it is not possible to abstain completely from any of these activities. Alcoholics are able to abstain from alcohol, and drug addicts from drugs. Historically, there was debate in the clinical literature about whether total abstinence was an essential goal for substance abusers, or whether they could learn to become "controlled users." Later research (Ryan et al., 1986) found that addicts were generally not able to limit their substance use to small amounts, and advocated total abstinence as the treatment of choice. Yet food, sex and love, and shopping addicts have to develop some type of "controlled use."

Some of the female sex and love addicts reported difficulties with alcohol and drug use: generally they used these substances at the invitation of their sex partners and not when they were alone. Women were typically offered alcohol and/or drugs as a way of enhancing the possibility of sexual responsiveness. Often they compliantly used the substances, in an effort to please their partners or because they felt coerced by partners who insisted on not drinking or using drugs alone. Some women, especially those who had been raised in a strict, morally rigid, and guilt-ridden family, tended to seek an altered state of consciousness, such as produced by alcohol or drugs, so that they would not have to accept full responsibility for their sexual behaviors, which could be blamed on the substance rather than on personal desire. Some women found that drugs, including alcohol, enhanced their enjoyment of sex, and so they became addicted to both.

Female sex and love addicts tended to become involved with other sex and love addicts or with partners who were addicted to substances. Their partners tended to be in denial of their addictions. Two sex and love addicts involved with each other tended to intensify the level of melodrama and obsession. Thus, co-addictive behaviors were exhibited concurrently with addictive behaviors.

PREGNANCY RISK

I was concerned when I realized that the women were spending part of every group session talking about fears of pregnancy, and of course they were obsessing over these fears even more in their daily thoughts; the men in the groups never mentioned fears that their female partners might become pregnant. Thus, the concern with pregnancy in the addicted population was still falling exclusively upon the women. In fact, the women who were having unprotected sex reported either no concern from their partners or unrealistic comments from the men that a pregnancy might enhance the romance or the woman's life in general.

The risks of pregnancy, AIDS (acquired immune deficiency syndrome), and venereal diseases can be viewed from a number of perspectives. They illustrate the self-destructive behaviors so typical of addictions in general. They also emphasize the great degree to which reality becomes distorted when the clients are acting out their addiction: the tremendous denial exhibited by engaging in unprotected sex. The description of a client's ("Barbara") first sexual intercourse with a new partner illustrates the flavor of this denial. Barbara stated with little affect: "He was making love to me, and suddenly was inside me. Afterward, he said, 'Were you using any contraception . . . because I just came inside of you.' " This woman had previously told her partner that it was important to use condoms because of AIDS, and asked if he had been tested for AIDS. Also, Barbara's lover was married. It was dramatically evident to me that the man was highly inconsiderate of (and, at least unconsciously, hostile toward) Barbara, his wife, and ultimately himself. Yet Barbara felt impressed with him: "He was so considerate toward me. When we took a shower afterward, he put a towel on the floor for me to step on, and handed me another towel to dry myself with."

Fear of pregnancy sometimes became its own obsession. The repeated drama of unprotected sex, and the intense worrying that followed, was particularly evident with one woman. I asked her to describe other times when she had worried about pregnancy, only to learn that as a child, she had been terribly worried that she might be pregnant after her brother started having intercourse with her. When her period was late, she wanted to die, and jumped out a window. She survived, but bled, and never figured out if she had miscarried or just bled from injuries. In her current behavior, she was compulsively reliving this trauma over and over. After reexperiencing and integrating the traumatic feelings within the context of the group, she was able shortly afterward to insist to her partner that they would engage only in "safe(r) sex." This action greatly boosted her self-esteem and initiated a positive cycle in her recovery.

CHILDHOOD SEXUAL ABUSE AND INCEST ISSUES

Sex and love addiction has been linked to a history of childhood sexual abuse and incest. Patrick Carnes (1983) wrote that sex and love addiction is a disease which is not actually about sex but about great pain. He stressed the necessity for a full exploration of the possibility of earlier sexual abuse because some clients have been so traumatized and there has been so much denial of their abuse that they do not realize that they have been sexually abused. Specific questions about things that may have happened are much more helpful than asking clients if they have been incested or abused. Emotional incest (Love, 1990), when children are used to satisfy parental needs that should be satisfied by other adults while the children's needs are ignored, can also be an etiological factor in addiction. Living with an untreated sex- and love-addicted parent can be sexually abusive to children because of the distorted messages about the meaning of sex, unpredictable behavior and emotional unavailability of the parent, and denial and dishonesty in the family.

Sometimes I felt there was no difference between my group and incest survivor groups, except that my group members had the awareness that something was wrong with their sexual behaviors as adults. In Philadelphia, there is a meeting of SLAA that focuses each week on the subject of incest, leading its members to introduce themselves as both sex and love addicts, and incest survivors. I encouraged my group members to attend this particular meeting. There are enough sex and love addicts in Philadelphia to fill many such meetings.

Earlier in this chapter, I referred to a client who allowed her lover's brother to live with them. During her hospitalization, she remembered instances of sibling incest and, from a hospital phone, she confronted her family with these memories. During a subsequent family session, her mother complained that her daughter seemed to be blaming her problems on what happened with her brother, when in fact she had problems and was "boy crazy" before the incidents with her brother. The mother said this in such a convincing way that even I felt confused. I asked the client in the next session if she had ever been touched sexually before her brother touched her, and she denied it. Denial in this family was manifested in the mother's need to identify her daughter as the patient, to idolize her son, and to dismiss her husband's alcoholism as a possible etiological factor in her daughter's addiction. She later told the daughter to seek help from a psychiatrist for her psychiatric problems, and rejected the idea that her daughter was sex- and love-addicted.

It was striking to me that this client, who had been incested by her brother, came to believe that she loved two brothers, especially after she agreed to her lover's emotionally confusing request to allow his brother to watch them making love. During her period of involvement with the brothers, she also seemed to be quite emotionally involved with other family members and friends. The father of the brothers had a fight with her and his sons, which resulted in his smashing her car window and threatening his sons with a gun. She developed feelings of closeness with the mother, who was in her age range and had been involved with younger men, and she obsessed and agonized over what the mother felt toward her. The mother's current boyfriend also lived with my client and the two brothers for a brief time, during which he both proposed marriage to my client and stole checks from her.

It was well worth the time in the group therapy discussions to closely examine the complex network of relationships that was sometimes part of the romantic involvement, including multiple sexual/emotional intrigues with family members and friends of their partners and/or former lovers. Exploration of the feelings associated with these networked relationships proved fruitful in uncovering feelings related to childhood physical, emotional, and sexual abuse, and often suggested an unconscious reenactment of incestuous trauma.

SEPARATION/INDIVIDUATION ISSUES

The women tended to remain very emotionally involved with their families of origin, who often appeared to be co-dependent in their attempt to control many of their sexual activities, child care behaviors, employment, housing, and other behaviors. Some of the women still lived with their parents. At times, it seemed to be as important to explore separation/individuation issues with the family of origin as to explore addiction-related behaviors and feelings.

When the women became involved in successive romantic relationships, they tended to mimic their difficulties in emotionally separating from their families of origin: they tended never to completely break off these relationships. Whether the clients were being treated for sex and love addiction or co-addiction, they all continued to have relationships with former boyfriends. At unexpected times, sometimes even years later, the men would suddenly reappear in their lives, resulting in anything from a brief sexual fling to a nonsexual involvement to a full-blown obsessive relationship. At other times, the women reinitiated the contact with former partners during times of loneliness or desperation.

These "dangling" relationships can be viewed as sexual/romantic "intrigues" or as a type of "stash" for possible use in the future. Keeping a book with names, addresses, and phone numbers of former lovers was analogous to an alcoholic's keeping a few bottles hidden in his/her apartment. Just as a relapse for an alcoholic might begin at the moment of remembering the location of the hidden bottle, so the relapse for a sex and love addict might begin at the moment of feeling excitement that it is possible to contact a former lover.

Another way in which difficulties with separation/individuation issues tended to resurface was in the group members' relationship with each other and with me. There sometimes were attempts to have inappropriate relationships with me. These included a woman having an intense fantasy about living with me (after just two sessions), and a woman calling me in the middle of the night to ask if she could come over. Women also had termination difficulties. One woman stopped coming a week at a time, offering various excuses, until she finally said that she did not want to come for an indefinite period of time. She refused my invitation to come to the group for a termination session. Another woman said that she would not be able to come for four to six weeks. When I called her after that time, she acted as though I should have understood that she was never coming back.

The separation/individuation difficulties evident within the group context yielded clues for understanding the ways in which the normal development of separation/individuation from the family of origin had been thwarted. For example, one woman would live periodically on her own and then with her parents. When she lived on her own, she tended to withdraw completely from contact with her parents; when she lived with them, she allowed them to control many of her behaviors, even giving them her money so they could pay her bills. This same client went through periods of ambivalence about being a group member, leaving the group and returning to it. The group had the therapeutic value of offering the opportunity to establish appropriate boundaries, which might serve as a corrective emotional experience and help clients to develop better relationships with their families and friends.

THE CHALLENGE OF USING RELATIONSHIP-BASED THERAPY TO DEAL WITH RELATIONSHIP ISSUES

Considering that sex- and love-addicted/dependent women and men establish relationships that are dysfunctional, it becomes quite a paradox to treat them in the context of relationship-based individual and/or group therapy. Thus, the difficulties of engaging in and terminating the therapeutic relationship are not surprising. Yet the possibility is great for individual healing to occur within a therapeutic group. Opportunities are provided for healthy relationships with the group leader and with the other group members, which (it is hoped) can later be transferred to other relationships.

Given a therapeutic philosophy where abstinence from sexual and romantic relationships is advocated on a temporary basis, it is essential to provide role models for healthy emotional relationships while the person is free from acting-out behaviors and can begin to explore new ways of relating to people. Most of the female sex and love addicts tended to have relationships only with male partners, often shunning relationships with other women. Just as it is recommended that alcoholics and drug addicts abstain from relationships with people with whom they formerly abused substances, it is suggested that sex and love addicts withdraw from unhealthy relationships. Sometimes it follows that the addict has no social community at all. It therefore becomes essential to form a new social network, which can be provided both within the Twelve Step meetings and in group psychotherapy. These group experiences are critical in alleviating the loneliness that is often so acutely felt by addicts when they stop acting out, and that leads to relapse if not addressed.

Society at large often sabotages therapy for sex and love addiction by (a) glorifying the sexualization of people (including children) and even of inanimate objects (e.g., cars and cigarettes), (b) tolerating a great amount of sexual harassment and abuse, (c) disbelieving accounts of incest and other childhood abuse, (d) generally mocking celibacy, (e) defining women by their relationships with men, and (f) glorifying men for the number of their sexual conquests. Thus, the sexual and emotional abuse suffered by the female clients in their childhood and within the context of their particular families becomes exacerbated by the unhealthy reaction of the society at large to their earlier victimizations. At times, the therapy group and Twelve Step meetings might serve as an essential haven for recovering people where healthy, nonsexualized relationships are fostered within the larger context of a highly sexualized and sexually abusive society.

REFERENCES

Bass, E., & Davis, L. (1988). *The Courage to Heal: A Guide for Women Survivors of Child Sexual Abuse*. New York: Harper & Row.

Carnes, P. (1983). *Out of the Shadows: Understanding Sexual Addiction*. Minneapolis: CompCare.

———. (1991). *Don't Call It Love: Recovery from Sexual Addiction*. New York: Bantam Books.

Chesler, P. (1972). *Women and Madness*. New York: Avon.

Griffin-Shelley, E. (1991). *Sex and Love: Addiction, Treatment, and Recovery*. New York: Praeger.

Love, P. (1990). *The Emotional Incest Syndrome: What to Do When a Parent's Love Rules Your Life*. New York: Bantam Books.

McGrath, E., Keita, G., Strickland, B., & Russo, N. (eds.). (1990). *Women and Depression: Risk Factors and Treatment Issues*. Washington, D.C.: American Psychological Association.

Ryan, W., Ryan, N., Rosen, A., & Virsida, A. (1986). "Practical Issues for the Clinician Treating Substance Abuse." In P. Keller & L. Ritt (eds.), *Innovations in Clinical Practice: A Source Book*, pp. 71–82. Sarasota, Fla.: Professional Resource Exchange.

Virtue, D. (1989). *The Yo-yo Syndrome Diet*. New York: Harper & Row.

Wesson, C. (1990). *Women Who Shop Too Much*. New York: St. Martin's Press.

CHAPTER 7

Integrating Sex Therapy
and Addiction Recovery

Stephen Heilakka

In sexual expression, the human being can experience a breaking down of physical, spiritual, and emotional barriers individually or with his or her partner. When the barriers are let down, at least three primal needs are being met. First, the inner child is reminded of nurturing received in infancy from primary caretakers. If that nurturing was not present in infancy, the inner child has the experience of having an unmet need fulfilled through the experience of being held and caressed as an adult. Second, the adult experiences a sense of confidence and well-being. There is a sense that a partner has been found with whom one can share the self and life experiences. Third, the soul is able to experience a moment of grace and unity that speaks to its desire to be reunited with its Creator.

It should be no wonder that sex is so powerful. At any given moment during sexual expression, the past (the inner child's needs), the present (the adult's needs), and the future (the soul's needs) are being expressed and met. At the same time a terror can emerge, due to the possibility that these needs cannot and will not be met indefinitely. This terror is the driving force in the sex addict's urge for sexual contact. This same terror drives the American culture's obsession with sex.

American culture is in search of an ethical and moral value system regarding sexuality. At the simplest level, the sex addict is expressing that cultural trait. Intuitively, the culture knows that sexual expression can be a healing experience. Intuitively, the sex addict knows that sexual expression has the power to meet primal human needs. Yet, in compulsive, driven sexual expression, these needs remain unmet.

If one surveys the sexual values of contemporary American culture, one must begin with the Puritan legacy, which has its basis in the religious mores of the founders of this country. Sexual expression was more an experience of sexual repression except in the marriage bed, and then only for procreation. This repression was further exacerbated by the Victorian era with its highly defined male and female sex roles. Such repression could only lead to rebellion, and in the 1960s, the culture experienced a "sexual revolution." This provided an opportunity for people to examine traditional values and judgments regarding sexual behavior.

Now, in the 1990s, one wonders what went wrong. The promise of "sexual freedom" is now limited by the fact that sexual expression with a partner can have life-threatening potential. What seemed to offer the promise of a sex-positive viewpoint has only increased the sex-negative viewpoint. In order to understand this phenomenon, it is important to understand the differences between sex-positive and sex-negative viewpoints.

The sex-negative viewpoint is concerned primarily with sexual behavior. As such, sexual acts are usually defined as good or bad in and of themselves. Whether participants in the behavior are active and willing participants is of no consequence. The behavior is bad, and there is usually a moral judgment attached to it; for example, masturbation is bad; premarital sex is bad. In addition, qualities of spiritual and mental health are often associated with the behavior, for example, masturbation is sinful and will cause insanity.

Characteristically, the sex-negative view holds a double standard for the sexes. Sexually active men are affirmed for their behavior. Though the behavior is not condoned, it is expected. Sexually active women are promiscuous. Their behavior is neither condoned nor expected.

At its core, the sex-negative viewpoint has as its concern control of the individual's behavior. At issue is not whether the individual will in some way be harmed by the behavior. Rather, the behavior is bad. Therefore, the individual who participates in the behavior is bad—for instance, having multiple sex partners is bad. Therefore, the person with multiple sex partners is bad. While the sex-positive viewpoint will not condemn multiple sex partners, it will raise questions with regard to whether the behavior is healthy for the participants (as will be illustrated below).

The sex-positive viewpoint is concerned primarily with the well-being of the individual. Thus, sexual acts are not defined as good or bad. Instead, a new line of questioning is explored. What effect does the behavior have on the individual? Is the behavior life-enhancing or life-detracting? For instance, masturbation is a pleasurable experience. Is it practiced in a way that enhances the individual, or is it used to numb painful feelings or avoid intimate sexual contact? If masturbation is used to numb feelings, what is the source of the pain? Characteristically, the sex-positive view does not hold a double standard for the sexes. Nor are behaviors linked to moral judgments.

This does not mean, however, that the sex-positive viewpoint condones irresponsible sexual acting out. It requires that the individual have a clear understanding of his or her behaviors and their ramifications. Exposing the self and others to sexually transmitted diseases is irresponsible behavior. Are the individuals practicing safe sex? If not, why not?

At its core, the sex-positive viewpoint is concerned with the individual's and the community's well-being. This is radically different from the concerns of the Puritan and Victorian legacies, which were more concerned with behavior than with health. It is also radically different from the sexual revolution, which was concerned with free sexual expression without regard to the individual or the community. Why did the sexual revolution fail?

The cornerstone of the Puritan and Victorian legacy, and of the sexual revolution, was the same: that sexuality is an act rather than a state of being. Viewing sexuality as an act that occurs between two people has obscured the natural developmental process of sexuality. The consequence has been the creation of a view of sexuality that has as its hallmarks sexual objectification, sexual dependency, sexual violence, sexual secrecy, and sexual shame. It should not be surprising that the sex addict's sexual experience is characterized by these sex-negative viewpoints.

If one sees sexual expression as limited to an act, essentially there has been a dissociation from the rest of the human experience. For the sex addict, his or her behavior serves the purpose of relieving tension through the process of allaying anxiety. The shared experience is not central to the sexual behavior. Rather, the quality of the experience is based upon whether there was an effective mood alteration. For the sexually addictive person, sexuality is defined as the act that he or she compulsively seeks out.

Culturally, Americans see sex as an act. Now that sexual intercourse is no longer necessary for the procreation of the species, thanks to the technological advances of in vitro fertilization, the culture is at a loss for a raison d'être for sexuality. What has emerged to fill the void is a value system based upon objectification, pleasure, and recreation. Again, sexuality is defined as an act.

Sexual objectification is culturally expressed in the sexualization of the human body for the purposes of relationship, whether it be a relationship to a product determined by an advertiser or a relationship to a person. In each case, the objectification serves to underscore the physical experience to such a great extent that the relational aspect becomes secondary to sexual expression.

If one views the human being as a sexual object, sexual dependency follows. The sexually objectified human being is no longer regarded as having value as a human being. Rather, he or she is regarded as an object responsible for the sexual pleasures of others.

Dependency emerges when the individual forgoes responsibility for sexual wholeness and is reliant upon a partner for it. The person who finds no pleasure in masturbation and is reliant on another person's presence has moved into the arena of sexual dependency. What is important for this person is simply that another person be present. The issue of relationship is disregarded. Interestingly, advocates for a sex-positive viewpoint often will argue that this behavior is not a dependent behavior but a sexually enhancing experience. It may indeed be a sexually enhancing experience, and there is nothing inherently wrong with any sexual behavior. What the true sex-positive viewpoint will do, however, is look at sexual experience and question the motives behind the behavior. Is it enhancing the whole person, or is it an expression of objectification and dependency?

The issue of dependency has been overlooked because it is the dynamic upon which marriage has been based. Women were viewed as objects owned by men, as objects responsible for the sexual pleasure of men. The male was sexually dependent. If his wife proved less than satisfactory, he was given license to seek other sexual partners. It comes as no surprise that the woman's sexual pleasure was totally dependent on the male. If the male was less than satisfactory, the same license was not granted to the woman. Not only was she supposed to remain "faithful," but the notion of a woman pleasuring herself was judged sinful.

Sexual objectification leads to dependency because it places the responsibility for sexual completeness outside the individual. If one needs a partner in order to fulfill one's sexual wholeness, the issues of objectification and dependency must be explored. Interestingly, the sexual revolution, which offered the promise of a break from this value system, failed. It failed to recognize what the Puritan and Victorian legacy failed to recognize: human beings are both relational and physical.

Prior to the sexual revolution, sexuality was to be expressed in a marriage relationship for the purpose of procreation. Today sexuality is best expressed in a relationship for the purposes of orgasm. The only change is that the goal is no longer having a baby. What must be recognized is that the sexual value systems before and after the sexual revolution deny the wholeness of the human experience. Human beings are both relational and physical. A functioning sexual value system must take that into account.

In addition to the values of objectification and dependency, sexual violence has become a key part of the current sexual ethic. Again, when sexuality is seen from the perspective of being an act, ever-increasing levels of physical contact are needed to fulfill one's needs. This level of contact may be expressed in increasing numbers of physical encounters or actual physical violence. In either case, the violence comes from viewing the partner as an object to fulfill one's needs.

What remains so curious about the current sexual value system in America is that for all their bravado, Americans live with a deep sense of sexual shame. It is as though sexuality is external to the human experience. Sexuality can be viewed in the movie theater, and while everyone seemingly affirms its wonder, the tenderest of love scenes receives an X rating. Sexuality has increasingly become associated with scandal in the United States; witness the increasing public fascination with the sexual escapades of political candidates and political appointees, not to mention the attention to the rape trials of national celebrities. Clearly, while the culture is willing to pass judgment and revel in voyeurism, there is not much support for attempts to come to terms with one's sexuality in order to make clear sexual choices. Instead, the culture lives in a state of sexual shame, unable to articulate sexual needs in order to satisfy basic human desires. While major sexual traumas continue to violate the human psyche—AIDS, abuse, unwanted pregnancy, and so forth—the nation continues to wrestle with the basic question of whether sex education should be offered in the public school system. No one wants to risk teaching a value system for sexual decision making. The consequence is an education system that reduces sexuality to an act between two people.

TOWARD A SEX-POSITIVE VIEWPOINT

In moving toward a sex-positive viewpoint, it is helpful to recognize that healthy sexuality is best described as occurring on a continuum. Sexuality is not an accomplishment. Rather, it is a constantly changing state. The continuum begins at birth and runs through the life cycle.

Sexuality is a developmental process that takes into account the physical, emotional, and spiritual capabilities of the individual. Every person is a sexual being with varying degrees of capability that are defined by the individual. One of the hallmarks of a healthy sexual ethic is that the individual is able to discover what is healthy. This means that throughout the developmental process, it is the individual's task to form a sexual value and behavioral system consistent with his or her current developmental stage.

As previously stated, healthy sexuality is not an act. It is a state of being whereby an individual consciously chooses to establish or expand physical, psychological, and spiritual boundaries for the self and with others. Healthy sexual functioning includes not just the behavioral component of sexuality but also the ability to recognize that the individual is both psychological and spiritual. As such, the individual is able to explore relationships with others based upon love, respect, and the absence of violence and shame.

While healthy sexuality acknowledges the importance of the physical aspect of its nature, at its core, healthy sexuality is essentially a spiritual exercise. This is not to say that the church should dictate sexual values. The church, more than any other institution, is responsible for the divorce of sexuality from spirituality and vice versa. One's attempt to maintain conscious contact with the Higher Power (Step 11) should not be divorced from one's attempt to embrace one's sexuality. Sexuality and spirituality both have the potential to lead to intimacy. Sexuality leads to intimacy with the self and other human beings. Spirituality leads to intimacy with the self and with God. Intimacy or lack of fear is a basic human desire. It is the lack of fear that sets the sex-positive viewpoint apart from the sex-negative viewpoint.

The sexuality model that stresses the wonderful physical nature of sexuality and then downplays the relational aspect operates out of a fear of commitment. The sexuality model that stresses the relationship and downplays the physical side operates from a fear of loss of control. The sexuality model that operates with the physical and relational aspects of sexuality being held in balance, through a commitment to the spiritual process, offers the greatest hope for healthy sexuality. This is precisely what the Twelve Step model of Sex and Love Addicts Anonymous attempts to do. The Twelve Step model to sexual recovery recognizes the pitfalls of the relational and the physical aspects of sexuality, and holds them accountable to the spiritual well-being of the person. What often is not recognized in the Twelve Step model is that when the spiritual well-being of the person is used to limit the person's full sexual expression, the recovering person's spiritual motives are questioned. The Twelve Step model encourages both spiritual and sexual integrity by encouraging the individual to explore making healthy choices. Interestingly, it is often criticized as operating from a sex-negative point of view.

HEALTHY SEXUALITY AND THE ADDICTION MODEL

The sexually compulsive person is faced with two dilemmas in coming to terms with sexually compulsive behavior. First, the male is culturally rewarded for sexual prowess; the female is rewarded for control. Second, the male is culturally rewarded for being the aggressor in sexual contact; the female is rewarded for being conquered. For the client to admit that his or her sexual behavior is out of control is to lose a major role affirmation (that being masculine is to be sexually active and that being female is to be sexually submissive). For the client to admit that his aggressive sexual behavior or her passivity accounts only for his or her needs is to lose another major affirmation (sexual expression is a right given to every male in spite of its impact on others, and sexual submission is the duty of every female). While the client's resistance to the notion that his or her sexual behavior is out of control is understandable, when the client comes to terms with his or her behavior, he or she can recognize the possibility of controlling behavior. It is this empowerment that enables the client to experience a sense of manageability over addictive behavior.

It is important to note that the beliefs about sexuality hold true for both heterosexual and homosexual clients. The treatment of homosexual clients requires, however, a solid understanding of healthy gay and lesbian development and the recognition that to impose the heterosexual model of relationship on homosexual couples is detrimental to the sexual health of the latter.

It should come as no surprise that a model of recovery which suggests that its participants refrain from sexual contact for a period of time should be criticized as operating from a sex-negative viewpoint. The invitation to a period of abstinence is regarded as being dangerously close to the Puritan and Victorian ethic of sexual repression. Indeed, it would be ethically irresponsible to suggest that one should refrain from sexual activity because one's behavior is "bad," be it compulsive masturbation, intercourse, viewing pornography, or whatever. What lies behind the idea of abstinence? Is it merely a cover-up for a sex-negative point of view, or is it a potential path through recovery?

Perhaps the greatest risk that is faced when suggesting that an addict participate in an abstinence contract, is the risk that the addict will move from a position of compulsive sexual behavior to compulsive sexual abstinence. This is often the case in the early stages of recovery, but it is precisely this pitfall that must be guarded against. To move from one extreme to another simply perpetuates the compulsive behavior. The purpose of entering into a period of abstinence is to provide a way for understanding and identifying the role that sexual energy plays in one's life. American cultural values maintain that people have no control over their sexual energy and, therefore, are at the mercy of the physiology of the body. The notion that one cannot have a sense of control over one's physiology simply validates that continued acts of compulsive sexual behavior are to be expected. For the addict, however, the question of what triggers the sexual response cycle is central to recovery. Perhaps the most powerful way to begin to identify the triggers is through sexual abstinence.

Claiming a healthy sense of sexuality is difficult for even the healthiest person. For addicts who have been victimized through abuse, neglect, and lack of sexual education, that task can seem impossible. However, with the support and guidance from other members of Twelve Step fellowships, a period of abstinence allows people to identify the nature of their sexual energy. Is it used to nurture the self, or is it used to numb experience? In refraining from sexual activity, the addict is given a chance to develop a sense of choice in the area of sexual behavior. It is the absence of choice that characterizes addictions.

In choosing to abstain from sexual activity, the addict is able to begin healing traumas that have been perpetrated by and against him or her. Patterns of reinjury, repetition-compulsion, and obsessive-compulsive behaviors are able to be identified. When this is done in the context of individual therapy sessions or group settings, the addict is no longer able to victimize the self through isolation. This act alone begins to heal the sexual shame that the addict lives with.

In group settings, the addict who chooses a period of abstinence is able to begin to explore, probably for the first time, the nature of his or her sexual response cycle. Interesting questions emerge, and correlations to childhood injuries are drawn. Without fail, the sexual behaviors of the individual begin to make sense, and one can witness the inner child's attempt to gain mastery over arrested sexual development.

Too often, complex systems are used to explain what are essentially simple cases of cause and effect. For example, in a period of abstinence a young sex addict who repeatedly put himself in dangerous situations with other men began to recognize that his attempts to be intimate with his father had resulted in childhood beatings. Now he was repeating the pattern but beating himself. Another sex addict was obsessed with pornography and recognized that it started as a way of coping with adolescent shame at being fascinated by the human body. For him, there was the avoidance of coming

to terms with his natural sexual curiosity through avoiding human intimacy and contact. The man who repeatedly injured his genitals suddenly
came to a memory of having his genitals tied up as a young boy. In each
case—and this happens more often than not—the sexual drive that was
out of control was suddenly recognized as a defense against painful
memories.

Sexual addiction can be viewed as symptomatic of childhood traumas.
It is a mask for sexual and emotional trauma. Sexual addiction is indicative
of a human being's attempt to discover intimacy. It is an attempt that is
gone awry.

The human sex drive is, at its core, a search for human connection. As
the culture has become increasingly less connective, the human attempt to
find that connection has become increasingly desperate. As community
has failed, as values have become obscured, Twelve Step programs have
provided a sense of belonging and community, a place for relationship and
intimacy. For the sex addict, they have provided a corrective experience
for an arrested developmental task.

Americans are imbued with sexual shame. It is a sex-negative heritage
that attempts to define normalcy as heterosexual behavior. The preamble
of the Augustine Fellowship strikes a blow at that heritage: "We are,
however, united in a common focus: dealing with our addictive sexual and
emotional behavior. We find a common denominator in our obsessive/
compulsive patterns which renders any personal differences of sexual or
gender orientation irrelevant" (Augustine Fellowship, 1986, p. 126).

To attend a Twelve Step sexual recovery meeting is to witness the power
of secrecy and ignorance being broken. People gather to talk and learn
about healthy sexual functioning. Attendees are encouraged to be honest
and speak with candor about their difficulties. To be homosexual or
bisexual is not to be shamed. To have participated in "sordid" sexual
adventures is not to be condemned. Rather, in the collective consciousness
of the group, there is a willingness to wrestle with the wonderful gift of
sexuality. There is a willingness to learn from the group. There is a
willingness to explore sexual sobriety.

In the handbook of Sexual Compulsives Anonymous (SCA), the following paragraphs are found:

In the SCA Statement of Purpose, we indicate that our goal is sexual sobriety.
This does not mean that we advocate celibacy, abstinence, or repression. Rather
our goal is to integrate our sexuality into our lives as a healthy element.

We use the term sobriety because of its deeper connotation of clarity of mind.

In sobriety, we are making sexual choices. In compulsion and addiction, we are driven and compelled into sexual behavior. (1990, p. 14)

It is to the detriment of the recovering community that the associations made with the word "sobriety" seem to be linked more closely to the temperance movement than to its meaning of being without excess or exaggeration. In its best sense, sexual sobriety is the state of healthy sexuality in which integration has taken place. Unfortunately for some, sexual sobriety seems more closely linked to sexual denial. Interestingly, sexual sobriety as defined by SCA allows for increasing awareness of the self, whereas sexual excess is a way of denying the truth of sexual or emotional trauma. Sexual sobriety acknowledges sexual energy as a part of a whole being and not the sum total of the being or the consummation of an act.

THE SEARCH FOR INTIMACY

At the beginning of this chapter, mention was made of the terror that the addict faces. In the search for intimacy, the addict is driven by the terror that the needs of the inner child, the adult, and the soul will not be met indefinitely. The miracle of the Twelve Steps is that they offer a way to heal the terror.

For the most part, though the desire for intimacy is primary, among addicts the fear of intimacy is also primary. Understanding that intimacy means to be without fear, it becomes clear that the addict is in actuality terrified of his or her sexual partner. The need to objectify and sexualize the partner demonstrates the established emotional boundary. It is the emotional boundary, however, that the addict wishes to overcome.

In the Twelve Step program, the addict creates a sexual boundary with the other participants. In doing so, a cognitive dissonance is created, for the addict must now relate in emotional, psychological, and even spiritual ways. Though this type of relating should be assumed as a part of healthy development in childhood, for many addicts this is the first experience of relating to people without expecting shame and judgment. It is the first step toward healing for many addicts because it is the first experience of intimacy: relating to others without fear.

As the addict cares for the needs of the inner child through intimate contact that is without fear, shame, and judgment, he or she begins to move into the next arena of sexual healing. With an established sense of self, the sexually compulsive person is able to experiment with nonsexualizing touch: shaking hands, hugging, and nurturing the self through touch that is both sexual and nonsexual. This is similar to the adolescent stages of human sexual development, in which the individual's task is to develop a sense of sexual well-being that comes from within. This period of development enables the individual to explore the personal sexual response cycle in relation to the self before moving on to relating to others.

The final stage of sexual healing for the addict is making a conscious choice to enter into a relationship. Having broken patterns of compulsive behavior that had been in place for years, at some point the individual decides that it is time to explore a relationship. Again, within the context of a supportive and nurturing community, the individual is able to examine, celebrate, and deliberate over what involves healthy sexual choice. These choices are not made under the influence of an external authority. Rather, they are made from a sense of empowerment that comes from understanding the motivations behind sexual energy and an understanding of the individual's sexual value system.

In the concluding paragraph of the chapter describing the withdrawal experience in *Sex and Love Addicts Anonymous*, reference is made to a "simple intimacy" that is discovered by the recovering person. It is the intimacy of knowing the self and discovering one's self-worth. From that position of strength the recovering person is able to go into the world. The addict has discovered that healthy sexuality begins with a self-love; that sexuality is a state of being conscious of and supportive of the healing process of the individual and the community.

REFERENCES

Anonymous. 1987. *Hope and Recovery: A Twelve Step Guide for Healing from Compulsive Sexual Behavior*. Minneapolis: CompCare.

Augustine Fellowship, Sex and Love Addicts Anonymous. 1986. *Sex and Love Addicts Anonymous*. Boston: Augustine Fellowship S.L.A.A., Fellowship-Wide Services.

Sexual Compulsives Anonymous. 1990. *A Program of Recovery*. New York: International Service Organization, Sexual Compulsives Anonymous.

CHAPTER 8

The Cultural Context of Sex and Love Addiction Recovery

Steve K. Dubrow-Eichel

They must needs go whom the Devil drives.

                                                        Cervantes

In retrospect, I have always obsessed over my relationships. My own growth, both as a psychologist and as an individual, has involved years of work on basic relationships. I never thought the content of my personal therapy sessions was terribly "unordinary." I also thought, over the years, that I had encountered all the major surprises my unconscious had to offer. About the first belief, I eventually discovered I was right, although not in the way I thought. About the second belief, I would find out that I was wrong.

Personal facts do not have to change; shifts in the way we perceive the context of these facts can bring complete redefinitions of specific aspects of personal history and identity. I spent years of my early adulthood searching for what I thought was the "perfect woman." My feelings about this search ranged from frustration to pain to humorous self-recognition. It took years of later self-exploration before I recognized what I now believe was my first experience with obsessive love and sex.

I met Karin (not her real name) in my senior year of college, toward the end of 1975. Our meeting seemed, at the time, unplanned and spontaneous. But I was far more "ready" to meet her than I ever imagined. Just before meeting her, I wrote in my personal journal: "Passion, that is the crux of the matter. . . . If anything, I feel ready, now more than ever, to find a real lover, to find a real passion" (Dec. 5, 1975). Karin and I fell quickly and passionately in love, and we experienced a whirlwind romance. Considering the amount of time and energy I spent thinking about her, being with her, fantasizing about her, planning on how better to "capture" her, it was almost a miracle I managed to graduate from college. On February 27, 1976, I wrote:

If I were to describe this semester so far, I would need to use only one term: passion. My feelings for [Karin] continue to grow and grow. I have never felt this way before; I came close to feeling this way, in part only with Beth emotionally and with Ann [not their real names] physically—never have I felt this way for one woman, however. When we make love, it is as if I would lose myself in the glory of it. It is amazing, literally amazing. *She becomes my universe, my God, my All.* All my awareness becomes concentrated on her and us. Never have I experienced such passion. An afterwards, when we lie together, I feel as though our bodies are merged into one. I am in a state of total bliss and peace.

At present I encounter sex and love addicts through two venues: my private practice (with children, adolescents, and adults) and my position as clinical director of a child welfare agency and residential institution for troubled adolescent boys. My own psychotherapy and recovery have become reference points for assessing myself and others. As emotionally difficult as it may be after all these years, I still think back to the way I felt, believed, and behaved 16 years ago to begin to comprehend the internal storms and passions of my obsessed and addicted clients.

Sex and love are the most available means by which we can seek not just to transcend but to escape, and ultimately disappear from, ourselves and our world(s). There seems to be mounting evidence that, as a race, we humans have an inherent need to experience altered states of awareness, to transcend—possibly even to "get high." Sex and love are—or can become—a person's primary mode of intoxication.

SEPARATE WORLDS: SHARED ADDICTIONS

I met William (not his real name) four months after becoming clinical director at the residential boys' home. Boys committed to the agency have been adjudicated delinquent or dependent (they are wards of the state or county welfare department); they typically are incorrigible, resistant, and emotionally disturbed. Our staff members are generally familiar with tough kids, but William was presenting unusual difficulty to the residential and social service staffs. Most direct clinical services at my agency are delivered by advanced graduate students in clinical psychology; because William was so difficult, however, I decided to take him on.

Arrogant, ruggedly handsome, an average achiever with above-average intellectual potential, William was committed to St. Francis after plea-bargaining on a drug possession charge. His height and stockiness made him look 4 or 5 years older than his 14 years. William was an exceptionally engaging young man with a finely honed sense of humor. What he lacked in physical attractiveness he more than made up for in personal charisma. He grew up in a working-class section of northeast Philadelphia; his father owned a waste disposal business, and his mother held various blue-collar jobs. William possessed a frightening temper, and he was proud of it.

William's parents were separated, and he had little contact with his father. There were gambling and sexual addictions on his father's side, and alcoholism and drug abuse on his mother's. William was himself cross-addicted to marijuana, alcohol, and sex. He had experimented with LSD, methamphetamine, and cocaine, but these were not his drugs of first choice. Prior to his placement at St. Francis, William lived with his mother and her boyfriend; his older brother was in a state Job Corps program, and his younger sister was in court-ordered placement, for chronic truancy and running away.

Drew (not his real name), on the other hand, grew up in another world altogether. The son of a wealthy New England physician with family roots predating the Revolutionary War, he attended exclusive boarding schools and an expensive liberal arts college, and owned the best of everything. Possessing exquisitely chiseled features and a body well muscled by the hard physical labor he enjoyed as owner and operator of a small construction company, Drew undoubtedly turned the heads of women and men wherever he went. I met Drew after he was discharged from a residential treatment and rehabilitation center that specialized in drug, alcohol, and sexual addictions. His history revealed a family background of well-hidden drug and alcohol addiction on his mother's side, and what seems to be a "socialized" or "episodic" sex and love addiction on his father's side. Drew's father has been married seven times.

FIRST SESSIONS

Whereas William immediately attempted to impress me with his machismo and bravado, Drew came across as the prototypical nineties man: soft-spoken, intellectual, caring, and gentle. During our first session, William made certain to mention his high tolerance for pain, and he bragged about being able to take any form of physical punishment. Drew was similarly dissociated from physical pain; during our intake session, he blandly described the events that led to his hospitalization:

I was working on a project when an electrical spark set some waste lumber on fire. While I was trying to control the fire, some wood exploded near me, badly scorching my left arm. I was so high on cocaine, I didn't feel a thing. Of course, I never really felt anything later on, either, and I didn't think I even needed to see a doctor.

It took a court commitment to get William to a residential treatment facility; it took a family intervention after an arrest for possession of marijuana to push Drew into a rehabilitation center. The nature of their placements reflected the two clients' ages and social status more than their dysfunction: Drew spent the next two months in a structured, well-endowed private hospital, while William spent the next two years at a child welfare agency that draws most of its clientele from families on public assistance.

Dissociation was a primary defensive strategy for both clients. Drew needed dissociation to survive in his family; his recalled history was filled with stories of emotional and sexual abuse, the former at the hands of his parents and the latter at the hands of an uncle and a cousin. Drew was able to identify these first, preteen sexual experiences as abusive, although he did so with no feeling and with predictably superficial statements about the need to "forgive and forget." In his early teens, Drew became involved in a series of superficial heterosexual encounters, usually but not exclusively with girls a few years his senior. Drew also indicated that he had on one occasion attempted incest with his younger sister, Alice (not her real name); she rebuffed him, and apparently repressed the memory until the family intervention session that resulted in Drew's first stay in a rehabilitation center. The intensity of that session sparked Alice to suddenly and painfully recall her brother's attempts; she has avoided any and all contact with Drew since then. It seems important and interesting to note that although Drew's initial abusers were male, he has been addicted only to heterosexual sex.

William had been physically and emotionally abused, but his sexual abuse, at a very early age, was very different from Drew's. Like so many of our boys at St. Francis, William spoke proudly of his initiation into sex at a very young age at the hands of a teenage girl many years older. I suggested, "You know, there are experts who would label your experiences as sexually abusive." William laughed, "Hey, man, then bring on the abuse!"

Therapy for the two clients was drastically different. Drew came out of rehabilitation with an intellectual, if not deeply emotional, understanding that he is an addict. William initially denied any difficulty with drugs, alcohol, and sex. He did not believe he needed to be at St. Francis. Drew could admit to his desire for therapy; for William, therapy was forced on him, and it would take months before he could consciously admit to a need and a desire for help.

And so my approach to these clients tried to reflect the diverse nature of their initial presentations. With William, I took a highly reflective, strategic approach. Borrowing liberally from my training in strategic/Ericksonian therapy, I used paradox, indirect suggestion, and subtle metaphors aimed primarily at helping William to achieve some level of awareness of his dissociation and denial. Kaufman (1985) discussed the etiology of shame-based disorders in a manner that, for my clients, seemed to round out the discussion of ego-state disorders and other dissociative phenomena studied by Watkins and Watkins (1979). Therapy with William often concentrated initially on "simply" acquainting him with disowned aspects of his self (his "alter"). William told me an experience he had at a party:

I was sitting down by myself . . . OK, I drank some beer, but I was definitely not drunk . . . when this chick comes over and tells me she just had to do me, you know, suck me off. So I let her, even though I didn't really want to, and didn't really like her. I just let her do it to me. It was really weird. I felt like I was floating outside myself, like I was watching myself getting head.

William was a chronic exaggerator; an initial fantasy he had about therapy was that we would trade sexual "conquest" stories. I considered the "objective validity" of his account to be of secondary importance; William's experience had thematic validity because it closely mimicked childhood abuse experiences. Rather than deal with whether this experience "really" happened, I engaged William in a somewhat successful consideration of the dissociative and nonvolitional qualities of this disowned aspect of his self. We concentrated on his feelings of anger, humiliation, and powerlessness. For several weeks, I did not attempt to connect his feelings with those he may have sparked in the many girls he "conquered." I used a strong accent and a dramatic hand clap to "mark" (or "anchor," as the neurolinguistic programmers would say) this story for future reference. I referred back to this story in many later sessions, and it became the prototype for a gradually emerging understanding of William's hidden self: his sex/drug addict self.

Drew, on the other hand, demonstrated a more subtle, difficult resistance. He could accept the intellectual awareness of his sex, alcohol, and cocaine addictions. Underneath his "psychologically correct" statements, however, was a deeper rebelliousness and a shame that spurred him to a quick progression toward what eventually became a major relapse. Fortunately, Drew managed to maintain enough honesty with himself and with me to agree to a contract in which we both defined a "bottom line" that would automatically lead back to a residential rehabilitation center. With Drew, I was careful not to feed into his constant, intellectualized self-criticism and self-victimization. I stubbornly insisted that neither of us could predict the shape and course of his recovery. Citing the research on nicotine addiction, I noted that sometimes several relapses were necessary before there could be a strong recovery. Over the weeks, I consistently reframed Drew's "failures" at "self-control" as "successful messages from the unconscious" that another stay in a rehabilitation center was necessary for recovery. (This was not a "technique" or "strategy," by the way; I honestly believed it.) All we could consciously decide is how loud the message must be before it was heard and obeyed.

When Drew came in the following week, he was able to admit that he had crossed his "bottom line." I sincerely applauded his courage and honesty. Drew then called his rehabilitation program from my office. Within four days, he was back in the program. Following his second discharge, he seemed more realistic about his addictions.

In spite of great differences in background, age, and therapeutic needs, the similarities between Drew and William were striking. Both clients were alienated from their emotions. William experienced primarily two feelings: anger (or rage) and excitement. (Interestingly as with most addicted or preaddicted St. Francis boys, sex and violence were essentially interchangeable. They are both forms of physiological excitement, and most boys I have talked to would have sex or get into a fight with about the same degree of interest.) Drew, on the other hand, felt primarily shame and excitement. He was largely out of touch with his anger. Both clients did not report feeling sadness or depression per se: rather, William complained often of feeling bored, while Drew typically felt either boredom or a vague kind of depletion and emptiness. Both clients used sex and drugs to transport themselves out of their bodies and into a fantasy world.

Both clients were diagnosed on Axis I as having an impulse control disorder, not otherwise specified (NOS); the additional diagnoses of dissociative disorder, NOS, and various psychoactive substance abuse disorders also seemed appropriate. On Axis II, both clients were diagnosed as having a narcissistic personality disorder.

Why do I make so much of the sexual act? Because I am a man without faith. I have no transcending faith, and fucking is the only means by which I lose my self-consciousness and transcend the triviality of my life . . . it is so short, this thing, this orgasm, so short. . . .

No faith, no faith . . . where can I find faith? I cannot search it out, that is obvious. So where can I find it?

These sentences, excerpted from letters written over ten years ago by another client, strike back at me from my professional past like bad memories of a secret crime I can never rectify. I treated John in 1983 for a variety of problems, but his primary presenting problem, I now realize, was beyond my expertise. Many of John's feelings and thoughts struck close to home, and I remember sometimes sitting in my office after our sessions, reviving memories and reviewing them with a new set of previously unknown doubts inspired by John's painful struggles. John was by any measure a professional and personal success. Married to a beautiful wife, with two children and a developing career as a personal computer consultant, John had compulsive extramarital affairs. I made many mistakes in treating him, including downplaying the connection he made between his sexual behavior and his lack of any coherent sense of personal spirituality. In fact, John was active in several antireligious scientific organizations, and he entreated me to join him in his rationalist attack on anything that hinted at developing spirituality. Like a good nondirective therapist, I accommodated him.

On many occasions, John would come to see me just prior to or following a sexual intrigue or encounter, and he would appear vastly different from the coolly "rational" man I saw during other sessions. Mistaking these states of intense psychophysiological arousal for his "real" self, I did what I was trained to do: I encouraged him to experience these feelings. I did not deal with these "highs"; I failed to recognize that I was attempting to conduct therapy with the equivalent of an alcoholic in the middle of a drunk.

THE PROBLEM

I need a means by which I can merge, by which I can prove to myself spiritually (I already have intellectually, but that is not enough) that there really is some cosmic beyond, and that I have the means to merge with it . . . perhaps then I could face, with courage, the triviality of my life, of my hopes, desires and aspirations—and of this analysis and psychology itself.

I wrote this journal entry on July 8, 1976. Beyond individual dynamics, what fueled John, Drew, and William? What fueled my own feelings in July 1976? Over the years, therapy has helped me to be increasingly aware of the roles played by my past and present relationships with my family, friends, and lovers. But there seem to be cultural and even species-specific antecedents to addiction and sexual compulsivity as well. Sex and love addiction exists within historical, cultural, and perhaps even biological contexts. A few key questions seem to suggest themselves.

Psychobiological Antecedents

Our first question might be Is there an inherent psychobiological need for transcendent or "peak" experience? Freud (1949, 1961a, 1961b) wrote of the universal enticement of the "oceanic" feeling that my have been our first primitive sensation while still in the weightless warmth of the prenatal womb. To Freud (1961a), the need to reexperience this "oceanic" feeling formed the basis of all religious experience; like dreams and slips of the tongue, religious behavior was a "normal" but neurotic "symptom" to Freud. He even directly compared religious experience with substance abuse when he commented on Prohibition in the United States:

That the effect of religious consolations may be likened to that of a narcotic is well illustrated by [Prohibition] in America. There they are now trying—obviously under the influence of petticoat government—to deprive people of all stimulants, intoxicants, and other pleasure-producing substances, and instead, by way of compensation, are surfeiting them with piety. (Freud, 1961a, p. 80)

Later writers, influencing and perhaps influenced by the renewed interest in human potential of the 1960s, wrote of the desirability of peak experience. Not satisfied with explanations that relegated religious and other forms of peak experience to the hamper of "neurotic" (i.e., "bad") needs, Maslow (1964) wrote about his experience with people who fear the emotional experience and potential shifts in perspective afforded by transcendent experience. He called these subjects "non-peakers," and he did not have good things to say about them:

[The non-peaker is a] person who is afraid of going insane and who is, therefore, desperately hanging on to stability, control, reality, etc., seems to be frightened by peak-experiences and tends to fight them off. For the compulsive-obsessive person, who organizes his life around the denying and the controlling of emotion, the fear of being overwhelmed by an emotion (which is interpreted as a loss of control) is enough for him to mobilize all his stamping-out and defensive activities against the peak-experience. (Maslow, 1964, p. 23)

From the 1960s to the present, we have seen a proliferation of self-proclaimed (and highly profitable) human potential enterprises devoted to the development and manufacture of "peak experiences." These enterprises, usually grouped under the general heading of "large group awareness trainings" (LGAT for short), employ a variety of structured techniques that feel spontaneous to the LGAT consumer but are in fact packaged and predictable. Many LGAT consumers report feeling "high" during and following these activities, and in fact go on to become LGAT "junkies" and New Age "cult hoppers" who compulsively seek peak experiences (Dubrow-Eichel & Dubrow-Eichel, 1988).

Biological Antecedents

Our second, and very related question, should be Is there an inherent, biologically based need for intoxication? In one of the most controversial books written about drug use and abuse, psychopharmacologist Ronald Siegel (1989) summarizes a great amount of drug research on both animals and humans. He notes that a large variety of animals seem drawn to, and even become addicted to, a variety of plants and naturally occurring substances that appear to induce a range of intoxicated behavior in their consumers. Many of these plants and substances appear to have the same, or analogous, effects on humans, while others range from being inert to deadly. But in general, Siegel argues, when animals are observed in their natural environments, and are permitted to self-administer drugs, their drug-taking behavior is remarkably similar to that of humans:

The self-administration model [of field observation and research] has proved valuable in demonstrating that drug seeking and drug taking are biologically normal behaviors. It has shown that drugs that are readily pursued by animals are commonly abused by humans. While selections of drugs by baboons and monkeys are closer to our own, most of these drugs are also self-administered by a wide variety of mammals, including rats, cats, and dogs. The ability of a drug to serve as a reward or reinforcer for behavior is not dependent on any abnormalities in the brain. Rather, those drugs that animals select to use are those capable of interacting with the normal brain mechanisms developed through evolution to mediate biologically essential behaviors directed toward food, water, and sex. In a sense, pursuit of intoxicating drugs is the rule rather than an aberration.

Since primates are the results of evolution's last days in Eden, it is understandable that the pursuit of drugs . . . among [apes, chimpanzees, and] baboons should be more than similar to us. (Siegel, 1989, p. 100)

In concluding that "intoxication with plant drugs and other psychoactive substances has occurred in almost every species throughout history" (p. 210), Siegel speculates that there may be evolutionary value to the attraction to intoxicating substances. For intoxication-related behaviors to be so widespread in the animal kingdom, especially in mammals, they must be "inextricably [genetically] associated with something else of survival value." Siegel argues, for example, that opiate receptors in the mammalian brain must have some genetic value; it "is difficult to think of [these receptors] as arising by accident" (p. 211). He also notes that behaviors which produce dizziness seem to be universal among all animals, and that dizziness is "a common aspect of drug-induced intoxication, and some drugs induce it better than others" (p. 213). For humans, the production of dizziness seems to be a goal of a wide range of behaviors, from religious dances and rituals to childhood games across very divergent cultures and times.

[Dizziness] is perhaps the most primitive form of intoxication and, aside from sleep and dreams, one of the oldest altered states of consciousness known to our species. . . . [It] is not only an ancient and adult form of intoxication, it is one of the first to be discovered by children. (p. 212)

Sex and obsessive-compulsive love do not inherently involve the use of psychoactive drugs. However, Carnes (1983, 1991), Griffin-Shelley (1991), and Lord (see Chapter 3 of this volume) believe that the behaviors associated with sex and love addiction do, in fact, trigger neurochemical reactions similar to those produced by many psychoactive drugs. Among my patients, I have noticed the same similarities between cocaine and sex addiction reported by Carnes (1990) and Lord: these addicts resemble each other when high, and their withdrawal symptoms are very similar. Of course, among addiction counselors in the field, the relationship between cocaine use and hypersexuality has become legendary: it is the closest thing to a "love drug" on the streets today, second only to Ecstasy (methylenedioxymethamphetamine).

Before moving on to proposing very radical solutions to the drug problem, Siegel (1989) concludes his overview of psychopharmacological research in drug abuse by positing the existence of a "fourth drive" (the first three being hunger, thirst, and sex). At this point, he seems to backtrack. Refusing to place the fourth drive on equal footing with the first three, he calls intoxication a "motivation" that is "not innate but acquired" (p. 209), although he doubles back again to note that "acquired motives such as intoxication can be as powerful as innate ones." He quickly reminds us that "animals will die in pursuit of cocaine with the same absolute determination that drives them in their quest for food" (pp. 209–210).

Of course, if we accept Siegel's proposition that intoxication constitutes a fourth drive, we are left with a weighty question: What happens when you combine two drives—sex and intoxication (whether innate or acquired)—into one addiction?

Cultural Antecedents

Few would argue with the contention that the years following World War II heralded unprecedented social and cultural changes in Western civilization. While some, or perhaps even most, of these changes—civil rights, the various movements for increased cultural tolerance, assertiveness, and minority self-determination—have been positive, there has also been a dark side to this upheaval. The disintegration of traditional cultural reference groups and social structures (with their replacements offering few improvements), the deterioration of stable, nuclear family groups and social networks, and intense difficulty making meaning out of rapid and overwhelming technological and cultural change have taken their toll on the Western psyche.

As traditional values (once thought to be universal, timeless, and absolute) have eroded, only to be replaced by a loose and vague marketplace of relative values and belief systems that can be bought, sold, and "tried on," Western culture seems to have become increasingly oriented toward instant gratification and immediate material gain. Near the eve of the "Me Decade" psychoanalyst Harbor Hendin and social critic Christopher Lasch produced two prophetic social-psychological commentaries on salient cultural trends. In *The Age of Sensation*, Hendin (1975) summarized his (at the time) recent work with patients drawn predominantly from elite universities in and around New York City. What he saw greatly worried him: as his patients moved from "a concern with revolutionary politics to taking drugs, to getting into graduate and professional school," he refused to join in with the chorus of social commentators who welcomed "a return to fifties materialism." Hendin warned that although "We would like to believe that the unrest of the [mid-1960s to mid-1970s] has ended and we can return to the relative tranquility of the past," there were "profound changes that have occurred in people over the past twenty years and have transformed the young" (p. 2).

Among these changes were an obsessive preoccupation with gaining and being in control. To accomplish this goal, Hendin's patients seemed to want "to escape their own emotions, to blot out, space out, blur, or flee how they felt about their lives" (p. 5). As a beginning psychologist, I remember how I struggled with the paradox of the obsessive-compulsive addict, the person who craves control but is essentially out of control. Hendin's patients seemed to live this paradox:

The students I saw tried many escape routes. The main ones moved in two seemingly different directions: one toward numbness and limited, controlled experience; the other toward impulsive action and fragmented sensory stimulation. (Hendin, 1975, p. 6)

Hendin also found that his patients increasingly were becoming ambivalently preoccupied with images of violence, death, and destruction; he bemoaned "the sense of death penetrating life that moves through the dreams and experiences of many students I saw" (p. 12). As I will discuss later, the use of compulsive sex (especially when it is combined with violent and misogynistic themes) as a means of magically controlling ego fragmentation and disintegration (death) has become a common theme in many of my sex-addicted male patients. At St. Francis, many of our boys are proud of their detachment from other people; they brag about how little they care about their girlfriends. This pseudo machismo seems to echo Hendin's finding that "for both sexes . . . caring deeply for anyone is becoming synonymous with losing" (p. 13).

For Hendin, the slowly unfolding pleasure of belonging, and the delicious unpredictability of true human intimacy, seemed to be giving way to a cultural ethic of intense, planned, and ultimately banal sensation for sensation's sake. This ethic would provide fertile ground for an explosive growth in addictive behaviors, although Hendin restricted his discussion of addiction to drugs, especially amphetamines and other stimulants (the cocaine epidemic was yet to hit, although Hendin clearly predicted it by implication). Still, sexual addiction is easy to include in Hendin's discussion of the unconscious rationale behind his predictions of increased addictive and self-destructive behaviors among the baby boomers:

You cannot be killed if you are already dead (numbness). You cannot be hurt if you withdraw (detachment). You cannot be completely wiped out if you divide your [psychic] forces (fragmentation). . . . We are a society which is bolstering the withdrawal of men and women from each other and providing social defenses against facing sexual war. (Hendin, 1975, p. 322)

Both William and Drew were clearly drawn to sex and love addiction as a means of temporarily alleviating numbness even while gradually reinforcing it. Not only were they detached and fragmented; the central defense mechanism associated with their trauma-related addictive behaviors—dissociation—served as a means of combining and achieving both fragmentation and detachment simultaneously.

Whereas Hendin concentrated on detachment, sensation, and manic avoidance of real emotion, Christopher Lasch (1979) took a somewhat different (if related) approach to what he perceived to be a growing and destructive self-centeredness in American mass culture. Thus, whereas Hendin analyzed society's ills using (DSM-IIIR) Axis I nomenclature, Lasch concentrated on Axis II. His diagnosis was narcissistic personality disorder on a societal and cultural scale. Lasch compared American culture in the 1970s to psychiatric patients whose "intrapsychic world . . . is so thinly populated—consisting only of the 'grandiose self' . . . the devalued, shadowy images of self and others, and potential persecutors—[that] they experience intense feelings of emptiness and inauthenticity" (p. 39). Like Hendin, Lasch characterized the need for (sexual) sensation in preaddictive people: "Chronically bored, restlessly in search of instantaneous intimacy—of emotional titillation without involvement and dependence—the narcissist is promiscuous and often pansexual as well" (p. 40).

Unlike Hendin, Lasch (who was usually considered a neo-Marxist social critic) traced America's growing narcissism to a political and economic system that increasingly objectified people and experience. He may have been among the first to write about the growing "psychospiritual marketplace" in which "pseudo self-awareness" was becoming a commodity. As a marketplace economy and its antihumanistic social and political institutions produced ever-increasing degrees of materialism leading to enhanced pathological narcissism, Lasch, too, predicted an eventual "flight from feeling" with an accompanying "sex war" (p. 187). He noted that the "decline of childrearing as a major preoccupation has freed sex from its bondage to procreation and made it possible for people to value erotic life for its own sake" (p. 188). The eventual, inevitable result was a false sense of sexual revolution. Rather than liberating, Lasch believed the "sexual revolution" would ultimately lead to increased objectification of sex, and therefore to decreased real intimacy and increased bondage:

Efficient contraceptives . . . and a "realistic" and "healthy" acceptance of the body have weakened the links that once tied sex to love, marriage, and procreation. Men and women now pursue sexual pleasure as an end in itself, unmediated even by the conventional trappings of romance. . . . Sex valued purely for its own sake loses all reference to the future and brings no hope of permanent relationships. (p. 191)

Lasch asserts an ironically overidealistic notion that sexual pleasure can be "an end in itself" for the detached, preaddicted narcissist. I disagree with this view. The person Lasch describes does not seem to me to be a simple hedonist. He or she seeks not just the sexual pleasure of orgasm but the escape and temporary transcendence even a dissociated "little death" (sexual encounter) brings.

Existential Antecedents: Sex and Love Addiction as Attempted Transcendence

> Most creatures have a vague belief that a very precarious hazard, a kind of transparent membrane, divides death from love.
> Maurice Maeterlinck, *The Life of the Bee* (1901)

> The orgasm has replaced the Cross as the focus of longing and the image of fulfillment.
> Malcolm Muggeridge, "Down with Sex,"
> in *The Most of Malcolm Muggeridge* (1966)

Having established a psychobiological (and possibly instinctual) basis for addictive tendencies in general, and for sexual addiction in particular, and having briefly discussed some recent cultural developments that may have facilitated the growth of addiction, it is time to consider the artificially transcendence-seeking nature of sex addicts.

Ernest Becker (1973) repositioned psychoanalytic theory within an existential framework, relying primarily on the works of Otto Rank and Sören Kierkegaard. To Becker, the problem of human existence was paradoxical. Trapped in a material body of limited durability, yet possessing a consciousness and imagination capable of transcending space and time, the "essence" of humanness seems to be man's "paradoxical nature, the fact that he is half animal and half symbolic" (Becker, 1973, p. 26).

We might call this existential paradox the condition of *individuality within finitude*. Man has a symbolic identity that brings him sharply out of nature. He is a symbolic self, a creature with a name, a life history. He is a creator with a mind that soars out to speculate about atoms and infinity, who can place himself imaginatively at a point in space and contemplate bemusedly his own planet. This immense expansion, this dexterity, this ethereality, this self-consciousness gives to man literally the status of a small god in nature, as the Renaissance thinkers knew. (p. 26)

Becker argued that repression was not the result of the resolution of the child's (Oedipal) castration complex but, rather, the result of the young person's growing realization that, to live without constant anxiety, we must deny death. All behavior, both "normal" and "neurotic," is on some level an effort to escape, postpone, and ultimately deny the inevitable. Because they are only transiently involved with the life-giving process of birth, men are particularly disconnected from Eros and especially governed by the fear of death. Males' fascination with producing and consuming material objects, and their apparent strong attraction to violence and sexuality, are among the more obvious reactions to the fear of death. Becker criticized Freud for refusing to "move away cleanly from his instinct theory to the more blanket idea of a death fear":

[Freud also] was unable to give large expression to the mystical, dependent side of himself. . . . But such a view is the seeding-ground of [religious] faith, or at least brings the person right up to faith as an experiential reality and not an illusion. Freud never allowed himself to step upon this ground. Eros is a narrowing down, in Freud, of a broader experiential horizon. Or, put another way, in order to move from *scientific* creatureliness to *religious* creatureliness, the terror of *death* would have to replace sex, and inner *passivity* would have to replace obsessive Eros, the drive of the creature. (p. 124)

Eros, to Becker (1973), takes on a more existential, even mystical, connotation; as I shall discuss later, it is the drive toward meaning, and the courage to face reality with faith and courage. Love/sex, then, rather than being an instinctual energy complete within itself, is in part derived from Eros and in part a derivative of the death fear. It is the need to transcend the paradox of human existence (infinite spirit/mind within a finite body) that drives man toward both religious and sexual experience.

Modern man fulfills his urge to self-expansion in the love object just as it was once fulfilled in God. . . . No wonder [Otto] Rank could conclude that the love relationship of modern man is a *religious* problem. . . . Modern man's [over]dependency on the love partner, then, is a result of the loss of spiritual ideologies. . . . Sexuality, which Freud thought was at the heart of the Oedipus complex, is now understood for what it really is: another twisting and turning, a groping for the meaning of one's life. (pp. 161–162)

Becker wondered if self-awareness, the unique aspect of being human, could become too burdensome, too painful to bear. In a society with no clear, culturally sanctioned direction or route to spiritual transcendence, modern man turns to compulsive sexuality:

Is self-consciousness [and] the sense of being a separate individual, trying to make some kind of meaning out of who one is, what life is, and the like [too painful]? Then one can wipe it away in the emotional yielding to the partner, forget oneself in the delirium of sex, and still be marvelously quickened in the experience. Is one weighed down by the guilt of his body, the drag of his animality that haunts his victory over decay and death? But this is just what the comfortable sex relationship is for: in sex the body and the consciousness of it are no longer separated; the body is no longer something we look at as alien to ourselves. (p. 162)

Compulsive sex is paradoxical: it provides a defense against fragmentation (cf. Becker, 1973, p. 33) between dissociated aspects of the self by temporarily uniting the self with the spirit, and the mind with the body. In so doing, however, it feeds the shame that ultimately powers a more ongoing, and ultimately damaging, fragmentation of the self. Compulsive sex is a perversion of the "Oedipal Project": the desire of the child to "control his own destiny with his own powers," to "conquer death by becoming the father of himself, the creator and sustainer of his own life" (Becker, 1973, p. 36). No wonder we find so many cross-references to control and sex in public media.

But why, then, does the sex addict feel so unsatisfied, with no apparent satiation point? Becker hinted at the answer when he discussed the nature of subjective heroism and its inverse relationship to existential guilt. In my opinion, had he taken the logical step of connecting the *compulsive* need for sexual transcendence to the experience of toxic shame and the trauma survivor's chronic reliance on dissociation, his theory would have been complete.

Psychological Antecedents: Shame and Dissociation

Shame, like its close relative guilt, seems to be inherent to the human condition, at least to some degree. There is a common colloquial distinction between guilt as the feeling associated with "*doing* bad" and shame as the feeling associated with "*being* bad." Shame, then, lies closer to one's sense of personal identity than does guilt. As harmful as chronic guilt can be, chronic (toxic) shame can be ruinous. Shame is more primitive than guilt; whereas guilt initially occurs in childhood when we violate an internalized, ideal self, shame initially develops in infancy, as a result of early interpersonal conflicts. The message from a significant other that we are "bad" induces the initial experience of shame; when that shame is experienced chronically, it eventually becomes internalized. This two-step developmental process, according to Kaufman (1975), eventually results in disowning parts of the self:

Shame inducement is the process by which shame originates directly out of interpersonal interactions in significant human relationships. Shame internalization refers to the process by which shame comes to lie at the very core of the self, and hence one's identity, and shame activation becomes an autonomous function of the self. There is no clear break between these two developmental events. Shame inducement does not suddenly stop and then give way to shame internalization. Rather, these are overlapping processes which can recur throughout life. (p. 90)

As these two processes continue, the child begins to defend against the experience of shame. "Means of defense begin to be tried out and, if sufficiently useful, develop into strategies of defense. Now we have a third developmental process also overlapping with the first two" (Kaufman, 1975, p. 90). Dissociation is one common defense employed when a shame-based personality develops. We know that, to some extent, dissociation is a learned strategy; it is passed from generation to generation. Kaufman (1975) hints at this process:

The important link between shame internalization and the formation of a shame-based identity lies in a process by which the self within the growing person begins to actively disown parts of itself, thereby creating splits within the self. It is the parental disowning of a part of the child, OR a part of the parent, I might add, which becomes the model for the self's engaging in like action. In a most fundamental sense, repression or experiential erasure and the splitting of the self into owned and disowned parts have their origins in the process of shame internalization. (pp. 90–91)

Again, observational learning is just as potent in this regard as is direct experiencing. The child need simply observe consistently enough how a parent disowns some part of the parent's self. When a child confronts a parent with an emotional truth about the parent, such as that the parent is angry, yet is met with discomfort, perhaps embarrassment or open denial of the child's perception, the parent is modeling the disowning of self. [It is] akin to what Sullivan had hold of when he described the "Me" versus the "Not-Me" or "Bad Me." (p. 93)

When toxic shame leads to the blocking of fundamental developmental needs from conscious awareness, "the experience of needing something becomes converted to something else" (Kaufman, 1975, p. 102). The experience of need can then become converted during an intense psychophysiological experience, such as intoxication or sex; it quickly becomes associated with the "high" feeling, and then becomes experienced as a "need" for that "high." This process would explain the "click" that many addicts have reported feeling the very first time they became intoxicated, as described in the "Big Book" of Alcoholics Anonymous (1976).

SHAME AND ITS RELATIONSHIP TO SEX AND TRANSCENDENCE

If the ultimate response to (toxic) shame internalization is the disowning of parts of the self (splits in the self), then sex provides the single best, easiest, and most available means of transcending the fragmented self. However, dissociated sex provides a circuitous and sardonic irony: in transcendence, the individual gets a brief respite from the internal dialogue of shame, and for a short time feels serene and integrated. But the integration is false, and soon after orgasm, the individual reexperiences shame redoubled. Like using salt water to quench thirst, rather than providing the much-needed and hoped-for reintegration of the self, sex addiction results eventually in increased shame, which perpetuates the splitting at the heart of shame-based disorders and the disowned self.

The typical compulsive sex or love addict embraces a deep involvement in an ongoing fantasy life. In my clinical experience, the intensity of, and importance placed on, fantasy may significantly differentiate sex/love addiction from other addictions. Preoccupation and fantasy, as vital components of sex and love addiction, are the connecting points, the processes that unite the antecedent forces (shame, dissociation, and the need for intoxication and transcendence). Griffin-Shelley (1991) would seem to agree:

Excessive amounts of preoccupation and fantasy can actually produce a trance-like state, especially when combined with rituals. This trance-like state intensifies the addict's tendency to objectify people and to numb his or her own emotions. (p. 25)

CONCLUSIONS

> Religion is the sign of the oppressed creature . . . it is the opium of the masses.
>
> Karl Marx

> Sexuality is the lyricism of the masses.
>
> Charles Baudelaire

It certainly takes a different perspective to view obsessive/compulsive love and sex as a "problem." As a society, our attitude toward obsessive/compulsive love and sex is, to say the least, ambivalent. We fear it, desire it, and have devoted a considerable amount of our artistic heritage to considering it. My own experience has not been unusual: who among us has not experienced, at some point or another, an obsessive love affair?

I initially posited the question of how we get to this point. While the forces that direct an individual toward sex and love addiction are ultimately unique, the forces that make an entire society vulnerable seem deeply rooted in both psychobiology and culture.

As intoxicants, sex and love are the perfect drugs. A few years ago, at a regional conference for psychologists, I asked the audience to consider this: a master chemist with unlimited resources (and a questionable conscience) must develop the perfect mind-altering drug. To fit this rather large bill, the drug must satisfy the following criteria:

1. It must produce an intense, extremely pleasurable high. It must be so strong that people are willing to do anything, even die, for it.
2. It must be in universal demand, and appeal to the broadest spectrum of people, ages, and classes.
3. It must be plentiful, in almost limitless supply.
4. It should be easy to market and manipulate.
5. It must occur in nature. Artificial substances would be eschewed.
6. It must be relatively safe, that is, impossible to overdose.
7. It must be readily and universally available.
8. It must require little or no paraphernalia.
9. It must be usable in groups and individually.
10. It should not produce a tolerance, yet should produce a temporary satiation, lest it interfere too greatly with other activities.
11. It must be undetectable, so that users need not be concerned about drug tests.
12. It should be difficult to perceive as a "drug."

What substances or experiences other than love and sex could meet these criteria?

The adolescent boys with whom I work come from predominantly addictive backgrounds. In 1990, I conducted a brief survey to assess the degree of addiction in their family backgrounds. Almost three-quarters had at least one person in the immediate family judged (by their family caseworkers) to have a recognized substance-abuse problem. Over half the boys had used alcohol or drugs to an extent judged by caseworkers as indicative of an "abuse problem" or addiction.

These same boys have repeatedly shown a level of potential sex/love addiction that is a caricature of the sexual obsessiveness of our society in general, and of the underclasses in particular. In a perverse revision of

Marx's pronouncement on religion, compulsive sex has become the opiate of these masses. Their pervasive preoccupation with obsessive (and often aggressive) sexuality colors almost all of their thoughts and actions. Many report having been (by my definition, not theirs) sexually abused as young children by older girls and women. Unlike their peers who have been homosexually abused by older men, these boys report engaging in ongoing and regular fantasizing about these early sexual experiences. (Interestingly, they typically deny masturbating while fantasizing, since this is not "manly.") They talk of them with pride and excitement, often as part of a "come-on rap" to an older, female staff member. The majority of my clinical staff (therapists and advanced clinical psychology interns) are female; their clients have ongoing sexual preoccupations about them. These preoccupations feel very different from sexualized transferences reported in the psychoanalytic literature. These boys make overt sexual overtures to their female therapists, and they are often genuinely puzzled when their advances are denied.

What are these boys looking for? When a 14-year-old boy in court-ordered residential treatment sexually propositions a 26-year-old therapist, I do not believe he is looking for sex per se. He is looking for transcendence. He fears death and fragmentation. He is looking for escape. That same boy, if granted the choice, may at any given time opt for sex, or for getting drunk, getting stoned on marijuana, or getting into a fight. All these activities are means to the same end: a physiological excitation or "rush" that is another form of getting high.

HEROISM AND THE SPIRITUAL WARRIOR

There are important differences between "true" peak experiences and the intoxication experienced by sex and love addicts. Acting-out sex and love addicts dissociate, distort their thinking, and believe they are in control. Ironically, of course, they compulsively organize their lives around losing control, and in so doing, do in fact lose control. My own clinical experience with self-actualizing nonaddicts and addicts in recovery echoes Maslow's description of the "peaker" who does not dissociate but instead seems to become even more fully aware. These individuals sound less "stoned" when they "peak," and their experiences allow them not only to continue with life but also to improve it, often in new and creative ways that involve enhanced intimacy. True peakers do not compulsively seek peak experiences but instead seem to remain quietly and satisfyingly open to them when they happen spontaneously. In the meantime, they get on with their lives and enjoy the base levels of joy and happiness that they appear to feel most of the time.

The close association between chronic abuse and trauma, psychic numbing, and dissociation is now relatively well known. Toxic shame, psychic numbing, and chronic dissociation (Lifton, 1968, 1976) add to and complete the existential explanation of the need for transcendence discussed by Becker (1973). United in an individual who has experienced chronic trauma, these forces produce a psychospiritual barrier to the normal ability to truly experience the creative and complete loss of self that marks benevolent transcendence and creative bonding with a Higher Power.

It may be that all addictions are a perverse and extreme caricature of a normal process that otherwise integrates biology with spirituality: the intoxicating peak experience. This need is fueled both from "below" (the biological "fourth drive" toward intoxication) and "above" (the existential need for meaning and transcendence). For nonaddicts, periodic intoxications and/or peak experiences satisfy this need. If the need is greater, due to biogenetic factors, characterological/familial factors (caused by trauma), and/or cultural predispositions, then any program of recovery must do several things: It must address the need for transcendence, provide new ways to open pleasure pathways to the brain, provide for the development of a patient attitude far beyond the normal "detox" time, and lower expectations (you may never get as "high" again). It also must provide support and community, and insulation against a world that facilitates addictiveness and glorifies all forms of self-destructive intoxication while denigrating healthy, creative spiritual experience.

Thus, if we accept the proposition that some form of transcendence and even intoxication is biologically inherent to human experience, then our solutions to the problem of sex and love addiction cannot ignore the spiritual and even the heroic. It was Becker (1973) who reminded us:

Not only the popular mind knew, but philosophers of all ages, and in our culture especially Emerson and Nietzsche—which is why we still thrill to them: we like to be reminded that our central calling, our main task on this planet, is the heroic. (p. 1)

The recovery movement is not the only source of potential solutions to the problem of sex and love addiction. The growing movement among men to form new communities of "spiritual warriors" may also hold some answers for both male and female sex and love addicts. Bly (1990) writes about "finding the 'deep male,' " an essentially mythic, spiritual part of the self (p. 6). He calls for a renewed respect for traditions and myths that allow for initiation into a brotherhood (or sisterhood) of "interior warriors." These warriors are not imperialistic aggressors out to conquer (people, nations, nature). Bly states, "The inner warriors I speak of do not cross the boundary aggressively; they exist to defend the boundary" (p. 147). Keen (1991) more directly relates the need for a means by which men can become "questing pilgrims" who develop "heroic virtues" that allow them to transcend without becoming addicted to sex; bonding and religious rituals may then replace alienated, drunken orgies.

Writing this chapter, like all my writing, has involved a struggle for me. To complete it, I reviewed and pondered over a wide range of personal and professional notes and journals, and I read books and articles, some of which I acquired years ago and then promptly filed "for later." I battled with my need to arrive at some mythological "perfect integration" of disparate material. I berated myself for leaving out important facts or concepts of which I am not even aware. I had my moments of exasperation and intense joy, even transcendence. It has been quite a journey.

REFERENCES

Alcoholics Anonymous. (1976). *Alcoholics Anonymous.* New York: Alcoholics Anonymous World Services.

Becker, E. (1973). *The Denial of Death.* New York: Free Press.

Bly, R. (1990). *Iron John: A Book About Men.* Reading, MA: Addison-Wesley.

Carnes, P. (1983). *Out of the Shadows: Understanding Sexual Addiction.* Minneapolis: CompCare.

————. (1990). Silent Shame: The Path to Addiction. Workshop conducted for Brennan & Lawrence Associates, Princeton, NJ, April.

————. (1991). *Don't Call It Love: Recovery from Sexual Addiction.* New York: Bantam.

Dubrow-Eichel, S., & Dubrow-Eichel, L. (1988). "Trouble in Paradise: Some Observations on Psychotherapy with New-Agers." *Cultic Studies Journal 5*: 177–192.

Fossum, M. (1989). *Catching Fire: Men's Renewal and Recovery Through Crisis.* Center City, MN: Hazelden.

Freud, S. (1949). *An Outline of Psychoanalysis.* Translated by James Strachey. New York: W. W. Norton.

————. (1961a). *Civilization and Its Discontents.* Translated by James Strachey. New York: W. W. Norton.

————. (1961b). *The Future of an Illusion.* Translated by James Strachey. Garden City, NY: Doubleday.

Griffin-Shelley, E. (1991). *Sex and Love: Addiction, Treatment, and Recovery.* New York: Praeger.

Hendin, H. (1975). *The Age of Sensation.* New York: W. W. Norton.

Kaufman, G. (1985). *Shame: The Power of Caring*, 2nd ed. Rochester, VT: Schenkman Books.

Keen, S. (1991). *Fire in the Belly: On Being a Man.* New York: Bantam.

Lasch, C. (1979). *The Culture of Narcissism: American Life in an Age of Diminishing Expectations.* New York: W. W. Norton.

Lifton, R. (1968). *Death in Life: Survivors of Hiroshima.* New York: Basic Books.

————. (1976). *The Life of the Self: Toward a New Psychology.* New York: Basic Books.

Maslow, A. (1964). *Religions, Values, and Peak-Experiences.* Columbus: Ohio State University Press.

Siegel, R. (1989). *Intoxication: Life in Pursuit of Artificial Paradise.* New York: Simon and Schuster.

Watkins, J., & Watkins, H. (1979). "Theory and Practice of Ego-State Therapy: A Short-Term Therapeutic Approach." In H. Grayson, ed., *Short-Term Approaches to Psychotherapy*, pp. 176–220. New York: Human Sciences Press.

CHAPTER 9

Conclusions

Eric Griffin-Shelley

The exciting and insightful contributions to this book reflect the developments being made in the areas of sex and love addiction, sexual compulsivity, relationship dependency, sexual trauma and shame since 1987. The first ten years after the founding of the Augustine Fellowship of Sex and Love Addicts Anonymous in 1977 were highlighted by Patrick Carnes's *Out of the Shadows* (1983), Robin Norwood's immensely popular *Women Who Love Too Much* (1985), the Fellowship's *Sex and Love Addicts Anonymous* (1986), and Susan Forward's *Men Who Hate Women and the Women Who Love Them* (1986).

Since then, there has been an ever increasing amount of literature available, such as *Hope and Recovery* (1987) and Brenda Schaeffer's *Is It Love or Is It Addiction?* (1987). The next year saw Jennifer Schneider's *Back from Betrayal* and Stephanie Covington and Liana Beckett's *Leaving the Enchanted Forest*. In 1989, Patrick Carnes's *Contrary to Love*, his *Gentle Path Through the Twelve Steps*, and Ralph Earle, Gregory Crow, and Kevin Osborn's *Lonely All the Time* came out. The first book for codependents, Mic Hunter and Jem's *The First Step for People in Relationships with Sex Addicts*, also appeared in 1989. A companion piece, *Hope and Recovery: The Workbook*, came out in 1990. In 1991, Carnes's *Don't Call It Love* and Eric Griffin-Shelley's *Sex and Love: Addiction Treatment and Recovery* were published.

The books that have been published only begin to tell the story of the exciting and explosive developments in the field of sex and love addiction treatment and recovery. Twelve Step programs continue to grow and expand in all areas of the country. Sex and Love Addicts Anonymous (SLAA), Sex Addicts Anonymous (SAA), Sexaholics Anonymous (SA), and Sexual Compulsives Anonymous (SCA) are providing healing communities that offer meetings, sponsors, pamphlets, books, journals, retreats, conferences, roundups, and more for sex and love addicts who need support and understanding. Professionals are offering and attending conferences, seminars, lectures, and courses on local, regional, and national levels. Recovering sex and love addicts and professionals work together as part of the National Council on Sexual Addiction and Compulsivity.

All of these developments are built on the increasing acceptance and comprehension of sex and love addiction by both lay people and professionals. This is not to say that there is no longer any controversy in the field; the concept of sex and love addiction is still debated as a diagnostic label. Nonetheless, there is a strong core of support and an understanding of sex and love addiction that has found a measure of acceptance and is the underpinning of this book. On this foundation, we have elaborated the ideas presented in the previous chapters.

REVIEW

We took the common elements characteristic of other addictions, especially chemical dependency, and applied them to sex and love addiction. We found that sex and love addicts experience a "high" that is pleasurable and addicting. They exhibit tolerance, and need more and more to get the same "fix"; they also develop psychological and physiological dependence that leads to a withdrawal syndrome and the experience of cravings. Sex and love addicts become obsessed with their "bottom line behaviors" and find that they lose control and become compulsive with these sex- and love-related behaviors. They encounter "triggers" for their addictions; they also become secretive, leading Dr. Jekyll and Mr. Hyde lives to cover up their addictions. This double life leads to personality changes and reflects dissociative states. All of these concepts are described in Chapter 2.

The need for better, more accurate, and more official diagnostic classifications for sex and love addictions is elaborated on by William Lord in Chapter 3. He makes a compelling argument for the inclusion in future diagnostic manuals of behavioral addictions that are characterized by compulsion, tolerance, and withdrawal. In addition, he takes the self-medication hypothesis of addictions, which has existed for years in the chemical dependency field, and applies it to sex addiction. His thoughts on the neurochemistry of addictions, especially sex addiction, are fascinating and frequently elicit inquisitive and excited responses from audiences. His thoughts point to an interesting and challenging future as we further understand the physical, psychological, social, and spiritual dimensions of addictions. Further therapeutic techniques and successes no doubt will rest in some part of this basic understanding of neurochemistry.

The therapeutic armamentarium continues to become more sophisticated and specific, as Eric and Helen Griffin-Shelley try to show in Chapter 4's discussion of the uses of individual and group psychotherapy in recovery from sex and love addiction. Each modality has benefits that are becoming clearer and more precise for clinicians and laypersons alike. As our resources develop, we are able to be more intelligent and focused about how to use them. In some cases, individual therapy is best before group work. In other cases, a good experience in group will lead to the decision to use individual psychotherapy as well for some particular goals. Both of these are combined and integrated with approaches that include Twelve Step work, bibliotherapy, psychoeducation, and couples therapy. Not too long ago, recovering sex and love addicts had only self-help meetings, which were often hard to find, or compassionate professionals who were willing to struggle and pioneer with them to discover a remedy for their terrible affliction. Now we have many tools and hope that the future will see increased availability and exactness in the use and distribution of these powerful healing interventions. We will also hope to be able to begin to discuss our treatment and recovery failures so as to find new and better ways to help those who are suffering, as well as to assist their families and friends and society as a whole.

Within the particular modality of group psychotherapy, Jeffrey Kaufman and Linda Dubrow provide important new ideas regarding the issues in men's groups (Chapter 5) and women's recovery (Chapter 6). Kaufman shares ideas about group membership and identity as well as his thoughts about therapeutic group rituals, new expectations about contact outside the group situation, and the role of sexual abstinence in individual recovery and the group process. Each of these areas is significant and needs attention, study, debate, and understanding from professional and recovering people. His thoughts about shame are particularly insightful and thought-provoking, especially his concept of the role of father shame in sex and love addiction and recovery. The key role of the therapist's shame and the need to be on solid ground in this area are highlighted.

Narcissistic vulnerability and shame boundaries are crucial elements in any type of therapeutic work with sex and love addicts. Other meaningful contributions in Chapter 5 are the comments on the issue of closeness/distance, the role of dissociation in the group process, and the significance of mirroring in therapy with sex and love addicts. While many professionals may find validation of their own work in these concepts, they had not previously been addressed with such clarity and depth. Insights like these will further our compassion, understanding, skill, and hope, which in turn will improve the healing process.

Linda Dubrow deepens and broadens our understanding of women's issues in the revealing Chapter 6. As addiction treatment has grown, special populations have begun to emerge and get the attention they deserve. Not all addicts respond in the same way to any particular treatments, and the "cookie cutter" or "one size fits all" approach does not work as well or as quickly as an approach that takes into account the particular characteristics of the addict. For women, there is the controversy and confusion about whether sex and love addiction can be lumped together. Some women do not want to be labeled "sex addicts" when they clearly have problems with relationship dependency. The common elements need to be examined more closely, especially since most of the literature separates sex addiction and loving too much.

Another key problem for women is identification and resistance to treatment. This is not problematic to sex and love addictions alone, but it is a major stumbling block because women in our society are expected to manage relationships and sex better than men. Multiple addictions, especially the interaction between sex and love addiction and food addiction, is an important contribution and needs further attention from professionals and recovering people alike. In my work, I have often noticed the "yo-yo" effect between sexually acting out and acting out with food, but it was not until I read this chapter that these ideas crystallized. Likewise, since I work with men more than with women, I failed to see the issue of fear of pregnancy and sexually transmitted diseases with the intensity and clarity that a woman's view can offer.

Clearly, the areas of sexual trauma and abuse such as incest are significant in the diagnosis and treatment of sex and love addictions; again, further elaboration of these issues is needed and welcome. Finally, the paradox of using relationship treatments to heal relationship issues is a crucial focus for understanding and further work. As therapists, some of us intuitively know that this approach will work and are comfortable with the apparent paradox, but we need to be more analytical about the ways that relationships heal and the ways that we can become better healers.

Initially, there seemed to be a major clash between traditional sex therapy approaches and the sexual addiction model. In Chapter 7, Stephen Heilakka makes an important statement that endeavors to bring these two fields closer together. He points out that sexuality is a powerful way, as the sex addict knows, to meet inner child, adult, and spiritual needs. His thoughts about the combination of our Puritan and Victorian heritages with the effects of the "sexual revolution" to produce objectification, dependency, and shame, with the focus on the sex act rather than the sexual process of human beings, is both stirring and disturbing.

A sex-positive point of view promotes developmental, process thinking about healthy sexuality that also is present in the Twelve Step emphasis on relationships, spirituality, and recovery. In speaking to the integration of healthy sexuality with the addiction model, Heilakka points out that abstinence can lead to awareness of choices and of the individual's sexual response cycle, and does not reinforce Victorian or Puritan ideas of sexuality. The fear that the gains from sex therapy and sex education will be lost with the introduction of the sexual addiction model and its perceived sex-negative point of view should be calmed by these explanations.

Heilakka's strong statement that sexual addiction is a symptom of childhood sexual trauma not only echoes the voices of other clinicians in the field but also leads into his assessment of the potential corrective developmental experiences available in the relationship building and intimacy found in Twelve Step fellowships. He also highlights the shame, ignorance, and secrecy reduction found in self-help, anonymous programs. Finally, he addresses the search for intimacy, the development of appropriate sexual boundaries, the safety, and the nurturing of the inner child that are fostered in Twelve Step programs, which again leads to the conclusion that the sexual addiction approach is indeed a sex-positive view of sexuality and intimate human relationships.

The resolution of the conflicts between sex therapy and sexual addiction therapy offer a deeper, more integrated view of human sexuality. Like the other chapters, Chapter 7 points the way to a future where the energy spent in controversy will be better spent in the enhanced treatment of sexual compulsion and relationship dependency. As we reach new levels of understanding and communication among professionals and the recovering community, we will be able to forge stronger interventions that will ultimately lead to less suffering for all involved.

In Chapter 8, Steve Dubrow-Eichel presents a compelling and profound analysis of the cultural contexts of sex and love addiction. He begins with a personal story that I found courageous and revealing. Unlike many professionals, he risks some self-disclosure in order to encourage all of us to acknowledge our own tendencies to be obsessive about love and sexuality even if these were limited to our adolescence. He then shares with us his experiences with two sex and love addicts who come from entirely different social and cultural backgrounds and yet have much in common in terms of their compulsive acting out. They are both impulsive, dissociative, chemically abusive, and dependent on objectified, detached, ritualized sexuality.

Dubrow-Eichel places sex and love addiction in four contexts: psychobiological, cultural, existential, and psychological. He points out our inherent search for transcendence and "peak" experiences. Paradoxically, people seek control and live out of control. In his view, addictions promise but do not deliver on the quest to thaw numbness, to end detachment, and to reduce fragmentation. Likewise, narcissism and grandiosity can lead to escape and temporary transcendence through addictive acting out. Sex and love addiction, from the existential framework, can be seen as attempts at transcendence that are fueled by the psychological antecedents of shame and dissociation. From another perspective, we find the core issues of shame and dissociation are key to understanding sex and love addictions.

Objectivity about our cultural and social context is quite difficult for most of us. We are challenged by Dubrow-Eichel's thought to step back and ask ourselves how different sex and love addicts are from others in our society who may have other ways to seek release from finite limitations. Are we all so different, or is there more common ground than we thought? We are challenged to think about our assumptions and to examine the way we think about and treat people who come to us with problems of compulsive sexuality or love addiction. Dubrow-Eichel ends by speaking of heroism, which seems at times to be in short supply in our modern world, and offers the interesting concept of "spiritual warriors" who seek to transform and transcend our limitations and current levels of understanding. As we make these efforts to look into ourselves, our world, and those who suffer, we cannot help but grow in wisdom, strength, and hope that may translate into reduced suffering for sex and love addicts.

CONVERGING OF FIELDS

In addition to progress in the area of sex and love addiction treatment and recovery, we are seeing a converging of information from a variety of psychological disciplines. In particular, there seems to be more common ground being discovered between the treatment specialties of posttraumatic stress disorder (PTSD), obsessive-compulsive disorders, chemical dependency, and sexual trauma and dissociative disorders. The shared information regarding treatment successes and failures, techniques, theoretical underpinnings, and precipitating factors can only enrich the results for all concerned. We have much to look forward to in the coming years as we become more sophisticated about which treatments work with which clients in which situations.

During World War II, soldiers exhibited a syndrome called battle fatigue. After the Vietnam war, we noted that some of the soldiers made a poor adjustment to civilian life. After the traumatic experience of war, these young men suffered from nightmares, trouble sleeping, flashbacks, intrusive memories, exaggerated startle responses, hypersensitivity, anxiety, poor concentration, and problems with energy and motivation. The reactions seemed to be directly related to their military experience—for instance, some Vietnam veterans felt like they were back in the jungles after hearing a loud explosion like fireworks (a flashback). Having posttrauma reactions was quite stressful to them, and some could not readjust to life after the war. Eventually, clinicians defined their condition as PTSD.

Once PTSD became known, other professionals began to say that their clients suffered from the same type of disorder with the same symptom complex, but had had traumatic experiences like sexual abuse (including incest), sexual victimization (such as rape), physical abuse (like beatings), and emotional abuse (such as parental abandonment and rejection). In fact, many PTSD clients exhibited compulsive behaviors that appeared to be an effort to self-medicate, such as substance abuse, sexual acting out, and food disorders including compulsive overeating, bulimia, and anorexia.

Around the same time, the treatment of obsessive-compulsive disorder was refined and produced remarkable successes. Obsessive-compulsive disordered clients tend to be either "washers" or "checkers." Typically, clients with a hand-washing obsession will worry so much about germs and contamination that they will spend hours a day in compulsive, ritualized washing behaviors that may lead to severe physical harm (washing until their hands are raw). Compulsive checking of locks, doors, knobs, and on/off switches can similarly take up the person's entire life. Some medications, such as antidepressants, have been helpful, but the most successful form of therapy seems to be behavior therapy. Behavioral therapies will include an intense program to teach the person to control anxiety.

As their anxiety increases, people become fearful that it will never stop and that they will "go crazy" or explode. In order to interrupt this terribly uncomfortable feeling, they develop a ritual, such as washing or checking, that temporarily relieves the stress of their anxiety. Unfortunately, they do not allow themselves to go through the normal experience of anxiety that increases to a peak and then subsides. Consequently, they do not develop the internal resources to cope with their anxiety in a healthy way.

In behavioral therapies, clients learn relaxation techniques that allow them to engage their natural calming resources, their soothing neurotransmitters. Once clients have learned to relax, they are systematically exposed to small doses of the things they fear. At first, these are encounters through fantasies, but the most successful therapy includes real-life exposure to the things that clients fear most. Through this real contact with their fears, clients learn to use their internal chemistry to regulate their organism.

In addition to the therapies mentioned above, I was excited to discover in a recent trip to a local bookstore that there is a Twelve Step program for people who suffer from obsessive-compulsive disorders. It is, of course, called Obsessive Compulsives Anonymous (OCA). So, despite the existence of both chemotherapy and behavior therapy, some people who struggle with obsessive-compulsive disorder need the unique support and spirituality that a self-help program can offer. It had often seemed to me that addictions and obsessive-compulsive disorders had much in common, and the existence of OCA convinced me of it.

We have already touched on the developments in the chemical dependency field that have led to the discovery of neurotransmitters (see Chapter 3). The existence of these naturally occurring brain chemicals, such as endorphins, explains the "natural highs" that people experience while exercising, sharing, and making love. Learning to manage these chemicals may be what sex and love addiction recovery, PTSD therapy, obsessive-compulsive disorder treatment, and sexual trauma survival have in common.

Work in the field of sexual trauma has confirmed PTSDs for sexual trauma victims. In fact, this area of treatment has broadened our understanding of dissociative disorders, with the most publicity going to multiple personality disorder (MPD). While MPD seems to be an extreme response of the human mind to overwhelmingly horrible life experiences, the underlying dissociative phenomena are not so rare. In the dissociative state, the mind splits itself. A simple example of this is thinking of something else while driving. I frequently listen to audiotapes or plan my day while driving to work. I arrive without any damage to my automobile, so I must have accomplished the task, but I often do not have a clear memory of the trip. I do have a good recollection for what I was thinking about at the time. It is rather like doing two things at once.

I remember as a child being told not to try to do two things at once. I found this to be a challenge, and often sought to do more than one thing at a time. Sometimes this would end in disaster, but other times it would work. I remember feeling triumphant over those naysayers who said it could not be done. People who learn to dissociate may experience the same sort of confidence and pleasure at being able to divide their mental processes. Trauma victims seem to find this a necessity and learn the art of splitting parts of themselves off as a means of coping with the traumatic experience.

Addiction specialists are quite familiar with "split personalities" (see Chapter 2). Alcoholism counselors frequently hear from family members that the alcoholic seems "like two different people." Under the influence, the alcoholic can be a "rotten son-of-a-bitch," and sober he or she can be "the nicest person in the world." Drug counselors are used to hearing about addicts who are "house angels" and "street devils." That is, the drug addict is kind and pleasant at home but, outside the house with addicted peers, is tough, aggressive, and hostile.

One of our favorite stories is the story of a man with two extreme personalities: Dr. Jekyll and Mr. Hyde. We retell the story of the doctor and the murderer in one person over and over again. We seem to be fascinated by this dichotomy, and it probably reflects our own internal struggles with the good and evil sides of our selves. Rarely, however, do we think of our own tendencies to dissociate or of our own internal split between good and evil when we think of addicts or addictions. However, as some of our authors have pointed out (Chapters 5, 6, and 8), dissociation is a significant factor in sex and love addiction.

DISSOCIATION IN SEXUAL ADDICTION

In his 1983 work *Out of the Shadows*, Patrick Carnes describes the "addiction cycle." Prior to acting out sexually, the sex addict goes through a period of mental preoccupation or obsession. This phase is followed by some type of ritual. Finally, the sex addict acts out his or her particular compulsion. An example of this would be a sex addict who thinks of seeing a prostitute all day during work. After work, he or she drives through the pickup district, perhaps more than once. In recovery, he or she tries to identify the original triggers for the obsession and to get some support for resisting the temptation. He or she would most likely avoid driving ritualistically through an area known to be dangerous.

The obsessing and ritual lead to a trancelike state that is dissociative and enables the person to act out without immediate feelings of guilt or remorse. These come later and fuel the addiction cycle to repeat itself. Many of us have experienced healthy rituals that lead to positive outcomes like peace of mind. Attendance at church usually involves some preliminary mental engagement and is rather ritualistic in terms of behaviors. We usually enjoy a calm and pleasant frame of mind during and after such a healthy ritual. Regular exercise or getting together routinely with friends can be a similar healthy ritual that produces good-feeling chemical responses in the brain. Attendance at a Twelve Step meeting seems to produce the same results. There is most often some prior thought involved. There are rituals in the meeting that govern the transactions. People's frame of mind seems to change in response to the experience, which is at least in part a reflection of neurochemical changes in their brains.

In addition to identifying the addiction cycle with its positive potential for healthy rituals, Patrick Carnes, in *Contrary to Love* (1989a), has determined that the vast majority of sex addicts experienced some type of childhood trauma—sexual abuse, physical abuse, emotional abuse. This indicates that the capacity to dissociate most likely predated their sexual addiction. Sex addicts probably have PTSD and can divide their minds into at least two different parts. Self-medication through acting out (as suggested in Chapters 7 and 8) seems highly likely. People suffering from dissociative disorders and MPD tend to exhibit patterns of compulsive acting out with food, sex, drugs, alcohol, money, and religion. The probability of overlap in these two areas is striking.

THE CASE OF TED

I am currently working with a recovering alcoholic who identified himself as a sex and love addict about three years ago. His treatment as simply an alcoholic or a sex and love addict would be doomed to failure without an understanding of his childhood trauma and its effects on him. In other words, treatment professionals in the addiction field would have thrown up their hands in disgust because of his continued relapses and called him "constitutionally incapable of becoming honest" (according to the Alcoholics Anonymous "Big Book"). Now, with the insights that are reflected throughout this book, we are able to be more compassionate, understanding, and therapeutic with a person who needs a healing interpersonal relationship (Chapter 6) to resolve the pain of the past and to develop the coping skills necessary to tolerate his or her emotions and maintain healthy relationships with others.

Ted reported a history of severe physical and emotional abuse at the hands of his father that was reinforced by his abusive older brother. His father was a teacher and had a good reputation outside the home. In the home, he frequently became enraged with Ted and beat him unmercifully. Ted's father had been away from the family during Ted's earliest years, so Ted had an intense need to bond with his father and a fear of abandonment and loss. He remembers his father's utmost frustration when he would cry and "act like a baby." Ted's father and brother expected Ted to be tough and more traditionally masculine. Ted was an emotional and sensitive child who could not fit the macho mold that his older brother seemed to fill so easily. Ted described times when his father would "throw up his hands in disgust and say, 'I don't know what to do with you, Ted, go cry to your mother.' "

In sixth grade, Ted reported that his teacher noticed he had a "split personality." He can recall her speaking to him and to his parents about the two sides of Ted that she observed in the classroom. She saw him as being at times responsible, involved, hardworking, caring, empathic, sincere, and thoughtful—the essence of a "good boy." At other times, Ted was just the opposite—a "bad boy" who was angry, withdrawn, hostile, avoidant, closed, uncooperative, and difficult to handle. As his therapy progressed, albeit slowly, Ted began to trace his awareness of his dissociation and MPD to his abusive relationship with his father. The comments of his sixth grade teacher were a touchstone of validation—an independent assessment of the reality of his internal split—which helped him see that he needed to integrate his divided self in order to be able to recover.

Ted's road to recovery had been a difficult one. After he graduated from high school, he became an alcoholic in his mid- to late twenties. As his drinking became more intense, he lost his job, forced his wife to leave him, and eventually had to move in with his parents, whom he acknowledged "terrorizing" with daily threats to kill them.

He eventually found Alcoholics Anonymous and got sober in AA. After seven years of sobriety from alcohol, he had bought a home and had a secure job, a circle of friends, and an AA sponsor. However, his sexuality was a major problem. He masturbated compulsively to pornographic books, magazines, and videotapes that cost an excessive amount of money. He frequented adult bookstores and engaged in anonymous sexual encounters in them. These sexual contacts involved mutual masturbation and oral sex that placed him at risk for contracting sexually transmitted diseases and HIV/AIDS. He came to me for help with what he viewed as a "sexual addiction."

When I first met Ted, he had been attending Sex and Love Addicts Anonymous (SLAA) and wanted to join our outpatient group therapy program. He was not ready for the intensity and closeness of individual psychotherapy (Chapter 4). He joined our intensive group program and became quite close to another group member. He described feeling possessive of his friend, and was jealous and outraged when his friend talked to or socialized with other people (a form of love addiction—Chapter 6). Eventually his friend rather abruptly decided to leave the group and join another outpatient group therapy program for sex and love addicts in a different part of the city. Ted was crushed, and the abandonment and rejection that he felt triggered an intense relapse. He could not attend any SLAA meetings, and was acting out almost every week. At times, he had extensive binges that cost a great deal and threatened his job because he could not go to work as a result of his "hangover" from being out to late hours at the bookstores.

Ted entered individual treatment and got back on track in his recovery program. He developed a close tie to another group member and began to socialize with him. Unfortunately, his new friend developed cancer and became quite ill. Ted also found an SLAA sponsor—something he had resisted previously. Again his intimate relationships proved troubling to him. He got angry with his sponsor and took out some of his stored-up rage on him. When he apologized, his sponsor told him that he was, of course, forgiven and that he loved him. Ted was scared to death by this unconditional love.

At this time, Ted was acting out his dual personality by being the "good boy" in his recovery program and the "bad boy" at work. He had become enraged with his coworkers, whom he saw as self-centered, ignorant, and abusive, and withdrew into a private work area. He refused to communicate with them except when the demands of work required it. He disputed his positive annual evaluation and found reasons to alienate his rather tolerant and understanding supervisor.

At the end of the summer, Ted pushed himself to go on a month-long camping trip to the Southwest. He had tried to find companions, which he usually was able to do because he has many outdoor enthusiasts as friends, but none were available. In fact, two of the people he had hiked with had gotten married, which was a blow to his self-esteem since he struggled so with intimate relationships. By the second day of the trip, he was drinking again, and the remainder of the vacation was spent acting out sexually and with alcohol.

When Ted returned, he was too ashamed to continue his Twelve Step meetings or his psychotherapy. He again became a recluse. He did not clean his house, care for his pet, take out the trash, wash the dishes, cook, or straighten up. He drank sporadically and acted out with masturbation and pornography. Interestingly, he became much more active at work and came out of the private work area and into the common space, became close to his boss again, initiated new projects and cost-cutting measures, and showed much more enthusiasm for his work. When he finally came back to therapy, he told me he had noticed that he completely reversed his previous pattern: the "good guy" was now present at work and the "bad guy" was evident at home and in recovery. He felt safer this way.

Fortunately, since we had established a good therapeutic alliance, I was able to maintain some type of connection with Ted despite this severe relapse and regression. We are now able to agree that our goal for him is an integration of these two sides of himself that will allow him to feel good about himself and stop drinking and acting out sexually.

For Ted, traditional approaches to his addictions or psychotherapy would not have been sufficient. An addiction-oriented approach that could not tolerate periods of nonattendance at Twelve Step meetings or slips and relapses without becoming angry, rejecting, harsh, or abandoning would not have worked because of his childhood issues of abuse and abandonment by his father. A psychotherapeutic approach that could not provide enough encouragement to use Twelve Step recovery and the inherent discipline and independence of these programs without fear of his becoming dependent on AA or SLAA would not have been successful because of his strong obsessive/compulsive tendencies. An approach that did not take into consideration the contributions of those who have developed the concept of MPD, such as Kluft (1985) and Putnam (1989), would not be on target with Ted because of the obvious pattern of "split personality" identified by his sixth grade teacher.

The integration of all these approaches is what this book is all about. In the field of sex and love addictions, we have progressed to the point where clinicians are beginning to make use of the advances in other areas of therapy and recovery to enhance their treatment of sex and love addictions. Although there remains some debate and no "official" diagnostic category exists in any accepted form, clinicians are moving beyond this problem to more in-depth work with those who are suffering from this devastating disease.

In our work in the intensive outpatient program for sex and love addicts, we are seeking to move beyond the horizons of our current level of knowledge to integrate all that is useful and helpful for those in recovery. We think about and discuss the role of neurochemistry in the addiction and recovery process with professional colleagues and patients alike. Many of them help us to clarify and refine our ideas about the important role of biology and chemistry in the addictive cycle. We also dialogue about the form and pattern of therapy and recovery: Should this person have individual or group therapy? Are we addressing issues of codependency and their relationship with their spouse or partner enough? How can we help people to have healthier relationships free of any type of dependencies?

We ask ourselves and our clients to be aware of the special issues that men and women face. We look at these from a diagnostic and societal point of view. We try constantly to ask whether we are somehow blind to issues that may save the lives of our clients or of others we encounter down the road. We want to look at the interaction of addictions like the yo-yo cycle with food and sex. We want to be sensitive to the issues of pregnancy, sexually transmitted diseases, and AIDS/HIV for all with whom we work. We want to address concerns about childhood trauma, especially sexual trauma such as incest.

In our work, we call each other to be aware of the major role of shame in the formation of addictions and the destruction of the recovery process. We share with each other our reactions to father shame and try to keep an eye out for our own transference and countertransference reactions to our clients and their life stories. We use supervision and presentations to professional colleagues, as well as our own therapy, to keep us in touch with and on top of issues of shame from our own past.

We seek to be open to the wonderful efforts of our cohorts in sex therapy traditions that help us to keep a clear definition of healthy sexuality. We make an effort to use the developments in the area of "inner child" that seem to speak powerfully to our clientele. We try to challenge each other to present a sex-positive point of view that does not have leftovers from our Victorian and Puritan heritage. We talk a lot about the role of spirituality in recovery, relationships, and sexuality. We work hard to be clear about boundaries and intimacy with our clients and coworkers.

We continue to dialogue about the importance of such psychological experiences as PTSD and dissociation. We look for it in our work and in our clients. We seek to be open to the understanding of differing ego states, trance and ritual, and fragmented personalities like MPD. We talk about the impact of cultural experiences on our need for transcendence and about the ways that addictions appear to alleviate numbness, detachment, fragmentation, and pain. We keep trying to be as honest and as open as we encourage our clients to be in their recovery from sex and love addiction.

This volume is an effort to share with others some of our thoughts, experiences, and insights on this exciting and challenging journey. We are hopeful about this work, and find that most of our clients, lay contacts, and professional colleagues tend to share our enthusiasm as they come to understand this intensely captivating field. Sex and love addiction treatment and recovery are at a point of profound expansion, increased acceptance, and understanding. We hope that this contribution will help this process.

REFERENCES

Anonymous. 1987. *Hope and Recovery*. Minneapolis: CompCare.

―――. 1990. *Hope and Recovery: The Workbook*. Minneapolis: CompCare.

Augustine Fellowship, Sex and Love Addicts Anonymous. 1986. *Sex and Love Addicts Anonymous*. Boston: Augustine Fellowship S.L.A.A., Fellowship-Wide Services.

Bireda, Martha R. 1991. *Love Addiction: A Guide to Emotional Independence*. Oakland, CA: New Harbinger Publications.

Carnes, Patrick J. 1983. *Out of the Shadows: Understanding Sexual Addiction*. Minneapolis: CompCare.

―――. 1989a. *Contrary to Love: Helping the Sexual Addict*. Minneapolis: CompCare.

―――. 1989b. *A Gentle Path Through the Twelve Steps for All People in the Process of Recovery*. Minneapolis: CompCare.

―――. 1991. *Don't Call It Love: Recovery from Sexual Addiction*. New York: Bantam Books.

Covington, Stephanie, & Beckett, Liana. 1988. *Leaving the Enchanted Forest: The Path from Relationship Addiction to Intimacy*. New York: Harper & Row.

Earle, Ralph, Crow, Gregory, & Osborn, Kevin. 1989. *Lonely All the Time: Recognizing, Understanding, and Overcoming Sex Addiction for Addicts and Co-Dependents*. New York: Pocket Books.

Forward, Susan. 1986. *Men Who Hate Women and the Women Who Love Them*. New York: Bantam Books.

Forward, Susan, & Buck, Craig. 1991. *Obsessive Love: When Passion Holds You Prisoner*. New York: Bantam Books.

Griffin-Shelley, Eric. 1990. *Maintaining Sobriety with Bibliotherapy*. Center City, MN: Hazelden Educational Materials.

―――. 1991. *Sex and Love: Addiction Treatment and Recovery*. New York: Praeger.

Hunter, Mic, & Jem, a recovering codependent. 1989. *The First Step for People in Relationships with Sex Addicts*. Minneapolis: CompCare.

Kluft, Richard P. 1985. *Childhood Antecedents of Multiple Personality*. Washington, DC: American Psychiatric Press.

May, Gerald G. 1988. *Addiction and Grace: Love and Spirituality in the Healing of Addictions*. New York: HarperCollins.

Milkman, Harvey, & Sunderwirth, Stanley. 1987. *Craving for Ecstasy: The Consciousness and Chemistry of Escape*. Lexington, MA: Lexington Books.

Norwood, Robin. 1985. *Women Who Love Too Much: When You Keep Wishing and Hoping He'll Change*. New York: Pocket Books.

Peele, Stanton, & Brodsky, Archie. 1975. *Love and Addiction*. New York: Signet Books.

Putnam, Frank W. 1989. *Diagnosis and Treatment of Multiple Personality Disorder*. New York: Guilford Press.

Robinson, Barbara Lair, & Robinson, Rick Lair. 1991. *If My Dad's a Sexaholic, What Does That Make Me?* Minneapolis: CompCare.

Rossetti, Stephen J. 1990. *Slayer of the Soul: Child Sexual Abuse and the Catholic Church*. Mystic, CT: Twenty-Third Publications.

Schaeffer, Brenda. 1987. *Is It Love or Is It Addiction?* Center City, MN: Hazelden Educational Materials.
Schneider, Jennifer P. 1988. *Back from Betrayal: Recovering from His Affairs.* Center City, MN: Hazelden Educational Materials.

Index

About the Editor
and Contributors

ERIC GRIFFIN-SHELLEY is Director of The Recovery Center in Lafayette Hill, Pa., that offers the intensive outpatient program described in this book. He is also Director of the inpatient program at Northwestern Institute of Psychiatry in Fort Washington, Pa. He is a licensed psychologist and social worker in Pennsylvania. He is the author of *Sex and Love: Addiction Treatment and Recovery* (Praeger, 1991) as well as numerous articles on sex and love addiction, chemical dependency, adolescents, and clergy. He is certified in Gestalt Therapy from the New York Center for Gestalt Therapy and Training, and addictions counseling by the Pennsylvania Chemical Abuse Certification Board.

LINDA DUBROW is in private practice in Philadelphia, Pa. She specializes in sex and love addictions, compulsive eating and spending, phobias, and cult work. She is Director of Counseling at Manor Junior College. She has written articles in the area of cults and dissociative disorders. She is a licensed psychologist in Pennsylvania.

STEVE K. DUBROW-EICHEL is a licensed psychologist in Pennsylvania and is in private practice in Philadelphia where he specializes in sex and love addictions, cult work, and child, adolescent and family therapy. He is Clinical Director and Supervising Psychologist for the St. Francis' Homes for Boys in the Philadelphia area. He also co-founded RETIRN (Re-Entry Therapy, Information and Referral Network) for people adversely affected by destructive cults, satanism, and other manipulative social movements. He has written a number of articles related to this work.

HELEN GRIFFIN-SHELLEY is in private practice in Lafayette Hill, Pa. She specializes in treating couples, codependency, and women sex and love addicts. She is a licensed social worker in Pennsylvania.

STEPHEN HEILAKKA is in private practice in Spring House, Pa. and specializes in work with victims of physical, sexual, and emotional abuse. He is an ordained minister in the United Methodist Church and a member of their Eastern Pennsylvania conference. He is also the founder of Recovery Adventures—life enrichment and vacations for people in Twelve Step programs. He conducts a men's group at the outpatient program described in this book.

JEFFREY KAUFMAN is in private practice in the Philadelphia area and specializes in sex and love addiction and loss and mourning. He is the founder and primary program facilitator for the Center for the Care of Community Institutions in Bala Cynwyd, Pa. He is a certified death counselor and author of *Awareness of Mortality* (in press). He is the Coordinator of the outpatient program for sex and love addicts described in this volume.

WILLIAM LORD practices family medicine in Reading, Pa. He is on the medical staff of Reading Hospital and Medical Center and was former medical director of its detoxification unit. He is a Diplomate of the American Academy of Family Practice and is certified as an addiction specialist by the American Society of Addiction Medicine. He is a consultant for the group therapy program presented in this volume.